JOHN WINTERS

Self Discipline

Contents

Introduction

Here is the cold hard reality of a successful life. To live a life of meaning and significance you need self-discipline. You can't compromise on this. You can not achieve great success on this planet without a high level of Self-discipline.

There is a reason why professions where life and death are part of the job, depends on Self-Discipline. Jobs like the military, coastguard and others depend on the structure and stability needed to do their jobs efficiently and stay safe in a volatile world.

Normal Discipline usually gets maintained by some form of external threat or punishment from a commander or leader. This type of discipline is found at a lower level in a normal society with all its laws. Where if you break the law you go to jail.

This form of discipline at a very high level is common in recruit training in the military. This is very effective in laying a foundation of discipline in a short amount of time. The military then achieves the long term goal that the soldier will leave basic training with some sense of Self Discipline. Within the unit, discipline will build trust and order. This will lead to efficiency, confidence, and control.

Self Discipline is a higher level of Discipline. Self Discipline is where external threats are no longer the motivating factor for the following of rules. The person applying Self-discipline becomes the authority over himself. He is now the master over his own life. This type of discipline can be traced back to all great warrior traditions like Samurai or Spartans that approached Self-

Discipline as a way of life. Self Discipline was a code to achieve greater goals like Self Mastery. They knew Self Discipline leads to Self Mastery and that led to Control, power, and success.

Special Operations Units like the Green Berets and Navy Seals depend on Self Discipline. A lot of times the operators work alone or in small groups without any supervision. They are independent soldiers. That is why they get referred to as operators. The operators don't have an external threat of maintaining discipline. They get trained to become Self-disciplined. They get taught the value of Self-Discipline and they know that Self-Discipline is one thing they can always depend on. It's the one thing that will make the difference between success and failure.

These men succeed because they live by a code. The foundation of this code is Self Discipline. Self Discipline allows them to operate in extreme conditions and be successful consistently. This Self Disciplined code allows operators to be unaffected by external factors like death, danger, chaos, uncertainty and human coercion.

In today's world Self Discipline is very rare. The modern human mind has become very weak and fragile. The majority of people have lost control of their minds. They just go with the flow and have no mental toughness. They live with the mindset of the victim and have given away their personal sovereignty by not having any form of Self-Discipline.

You can just go on social media for 10 minutes to see the low level of physical and mental Self-Discipline. You see people complaining about being overweight and doing nothing about it. Or people being depressed and unhappy and not taking control of the situation. People having no money but spending the money they do have on garbage. People reacting angrily and waste hours on social media arguing with strangers because they don't have the Self-Discipline to control their emotions.

In today's world, we live in a strange environment where discipline and Self Discipline is seen as this alien thing. It's this thing that soldiers, athletes, and other professionals do but it's not something a normal person does. People buy into this culture of mediocrity and then wonder why they don't achieve anything of great value.

Self Discipline can be taught but it can't be forced like normal discipline. Self-Discipline can be encouraged. That encouragement I will try and give you in this book. I will share with you this fundamental truth. You are ultimately in charge of your life. You are responsible for all your actions. Everything that happened to you is your responsibility. By adopting Self Discipline and building a code of Self Discipline you can take control of your life. With this control will come a great amount of power. With this power, you can create any amount of success you want. However, you have to make a choice. A choice to start living by a code of Self Discipline or going back to mediocrity and driving into the shadows.

Just a warning before you start this book. This book is for people who want to be successful in life. This is the book is for people who want to go after life with everything they have. This book is for people who want to not just be successful in one area of life but be successful in all areas of life. If you are just looking for a book that makes you feel a bit better then stop reading now. If you are just looking for a book that will tell you how many push-ups to do and go on a diet then stop now.

This book will dive into the heart and soul of Self-discipline so that you can be successful in life. More importantly, it's about creating a culture of Self Discipline, It's not just something you try out for a while and then go back to what you were doing. It's a way of life. It's part of who you are. Or it's part of who you are becoming.

If you are ready to start transforming your life then keep on reading. I think you already made your choice since you are reading this book. So let's get started.

1

Why Are You Doing This ?

Why do you need self-discipline? Why are you reading this book? What made you study self-discipline? I get it! You want to get up earlier, go to the gym and all those little things that are all very important. But what is your real "why"?

Why are you doing this? The reason I ask this is that if you're "why" is not big enough then the rest of this book is not going to help you.

I see this a lot. Guys get a glimpse of motivation and they want to change.
   Or its new years again and everyone is making resolutions. So you get fired up and you start making all these promises to yourself.

You tell yourself I'm going to lose weight, I'm going to get my money right, I'm going to start eating healthy, I'm going to spend less time online.

These things are great. So you make your new year's resolutions and you get fired up. You start firing the first few weeks but gradually you lose steam. All that motivation you had just 2 or 3 weeks ago is gone. So tell yourself "Good effort but this discipline thing is maybe just not for me."

The Resistance

Here is the reality of building self-discipline. Before you start you need to go look at your why. Why are you really doing this? Those reasons I mentioned above like losing weight are cute and all but that's not going to get you to fully committed to what you want.

Because guess what?As soon as you start to change all kinds of funny stuff will happen. You will see friends beginning to question you about why you are doing this. They will tell you things like "I like the old you better".They will tell you "You are acting kind of weird" or "Come out drinking with us".They will fire all these things at you and test your resolve.

Most people, unfortunately, fold right here and throw in the towel. They break at the first resistance. Friends and acquaintances are just one form of resistance you will come across. There are many forms of resistance. The most dangerous form of resistance is internal resistance.

What is The Internal Resistance?

The author Steven Pressfield of the great book 'The War Of Art' gave it a name he called it the "resistance".The resistance is that voice that comes up when you want to start making moves in your life. It's the voice that comes up when you want to go running. The voice will whisper in your ear for example, "You don't need to go run now, it's cold outside, let's do it tomorrow. "

Or the voice will say "Go buy that pizza it looks great. Who needs these healthy meals you eat every night?" The voice of the resistance will be a constant pain in the ass. It will always try and stop you when you have important things to do.

Your "Why" Needs To Be Strong

Family, friends the resistance, and other factors trying to stop you are a reality. The reason most people stop is that they have a weak "why?".You need to go ask yourself why are you doing this? Why are you really doing this? There has to be something deeper driving you. Only you can answer this question.

Marketing secrets

In marketing, they have figured out that humans get motivated usually by 2 very powerful forces. The forces of pain and pleasure. Pain and pleasure by itself are just 2 things we experience on a daily basis. However, it can be incredibly powerful tools if you use them effectively.

In this book about self-discipline, we need something to make our "why" incredibly powerful. A great way to find your "why" is to go to the two powerful tools of pain and pleasure.

For example, why do you want to lose weight? To look good? Feel better? Whatever your reason is there has to be something more profound. Let's take pain as an example.

When you are fat you might see people pointing at you and laughing because you look fat in your t-shirt. How do you feel about that? Does it feel nice to be embarrassed? No, of course not. It causes pain right? It feels bad.

If this happens all the time the pain gets more and more intensive and severe.Instead of running from this pain how about using it to get what you want?How about remembering very clearly how that pain felt and telling yourself you never want to feel like that ever again.

So whenever you find yourself in a situation where you want to quit take a moment and think about the pain. Feel that pain deeply and then just get up and do it because the pain will drive you to get there.

For me, the pain was related to money. For a time in my life, I experienced so much pain with money that I would do anything to not experience that feeling of pain related to money. That pain became my "why". Ask yourself how much pain you will feel if you don't do that thing that you're supposed to do? Then realize you never want to experience that again.

Pleasure has a similar power although I find pain to be working better for me. If you want to do something for example not eat the cake then ask yourself this: How much pleasure will you have when you take your shirt off, and you look like an absolute boss walking around? Imagine the pleasure of the compliments and the admiring looks from friends and strangers. Imagine the respect you will get for being so dedicated to creating a body like that. These images in your mind of pleasure should be strong enough for you to get going. These feelings of pleasure will be your "why".

You Must Be Willing To Do Things You Have Never Done Before

After you figured out your "why" we need to get to a very important reality. This reality will make or break your attempt to become self-disciplined. Self-Discipline is a tool to live a powerful life. But it's also a tool to live a very successful life and achieve your goals.

For you to get what you want in life you need self-discipline. However, you will not succeed with self-discipline if you don't accept this important reality. The reality is this: You must be willing to do things that you have never done before. If you don't you will not be successful.

You are going to have to do many things you don't like. Therefore you will have to do things you have never done before. So you will be uncomfortable and you will constantly feel like you want to give up.

You Must Become The Ruler Of Your Own World

Most people on this planet are in an unconscious state of chaos. The world in its natural state is in chaos. When humans created civilization they formed a stable environment and brought some form of structure to the random chaos on planet earth. However on an individual level chaos still exists for most.

Most people allow external forces and their own minds and emotions to control and dominate them. They are not the masters of their own world. For you to get control of your own world you need to adapt Self- Discipline. If you are successful with this you will take control back. You will then find that you have a new reality that is built upon power. This power will be new to you. You will experience true freedom for this first time. Freedom from random events and impulses.Freedom from opinions, people and circumstances. For the first time, you will be the master of your world. You will be free.

Take Ownership

You have to take ownership of everything in your life. If you shift responsibility for what happens in your life to others you will keep on losing. When you are not responsible for what happens in your life then it means you are a victim. Victims are not in control of their own lives. When you take ownership of everything you will take power back in your life.

Going After An Ideal

We live in a world where 99% of the time limitations will be pointed out to you in the first ten seconds of a conversation. Let's look at two scenarios. I know you know the conversation in Scenario A.It goes something like this."I have an idea to start a new company".Your friend looks at you and says something like, "Yea but what if you don't make it or where will you get the money?"This conversation is an example of the most common mindset we live in today.

Let's look at scenario B, but it's one that you will probably never hear in your average day."I have an idea to start a company", your friend replies, "Well that is an awesome idea. Call me if I can help you with anything. I know you're going to be successful."

You have two scenarios; unfortunately, scenario one is the reality in which the majority of people on the planet live in. It's a cynical world where people don't like it if you go after something you feel passionate about or become highly successful in something you actually care about.

This is just one example of this mindset. It's not just something we see in our work life. It has crept into all areas of society. You can look at any area of your life. I bet you won't remember the last time someone totally supported you in the actions you take.

I remember telling one of my friends that I was planning to start a business. After I told him what I was planning, he reacted by saying, "Is that all?" Sure, I get it we need a reality check sometimes, but he could have said a thousand different things, however, he chose to be cynical in his first reaction. This is, unfortunately, the way many people react if you start going after things. If you do nothing and stay where you are, they are more comfortable. Then they will say nothing.

As soon as you go after something unusual or something that changes the status quo you will get resistance. If you quit your job and go after an entirely new career, you will get resistance. If you leave your church or religion, there will be resistance. If you move to another country there will be resistance, if you say you are turning pro there will be resistance, if you say you are going to be a doctor, there will be resistance.

Accept This As The Reality

Step one in changing your reality is to accept this as the reality of the majority of people out there. However, you have a choice. The choice is to get out of the Matrix (negative reality) and go after an ideal.

We have to go after an ideal. What does your ideal life look like? What is the perfect version of whatever you want to be? Think about your dream life and then go after it. It is our responsibility to step up and build a successful life. That is why we are here. If you want to elevate yourself above the masses of followers, then you have to go after an ideal.

What is the alternative? The alternative is going after a piece of crap that makes you miserable. And guess what? If you fail in the thing you love, you will be better for it. But if you go after a life you hate and you fail you will be miserable. Then you will look back at your life with regret.

Staying in your comfort zone and not going after an ideal means conforming to a mediocrity that is breaking the souls of men around the world.

You have to create your own sense of belonging by going after your ideal life. As long as that ideal is ethical and of service to your fellow humans. Don't go after something stupid, unethical or illegal that will hurt other people. That is not going after an ideal; it's going after stupidity.

So how do we go after the ideal?

Creating the best version of ourselves

As men, it's our duty to create the best versions of ourselves. By doing this, we serve not just ourselves but also our girlfriends, wives, partners, families, and society.

We can only be of service to the world when we go after our ideal. And this ideal is creating the best version of ourselves.

When I talk about creating the best version of ourselves, I don't mean being a little angel and acting perfectly all the time. We will still make mistakes and screw up. That's part of being a man.

By being the best version of ourselves means the following:

(1)Finding your purpose– why are you here?

Finding your purpose has many benefits, but one important benefit is that it might lead you to live a longer life. A recent study at Carleton University in Canada found some interesting results.

The results were published in Psychological Science, a journal of the Association for Psychological Science and it stated the following: "Greater purpose in life consistently predicted lower mortality risk across the lifespan, showing the same benefit for younger, middle-aged, and older participants across the follow-up period."

(2)After you got your purpose figured out, sit down make a plan on how you are going to go after your purpose

(3)Step 3 is to go after this ideal you created with everything you have and not let anything or anyone get you off that purpose

(4) Don't be realistic. I'm not saying do something stupid, but what you are dreaming might seem crazy or unrealistic to other people, but don't let that stop you.

I know about a lot of people who were "unrealistic."Henry Ford, The Wright Brothers, Thomas Edison, Steve Jobs, and many others. These guys decided they are going all-in on life.

This type of independent thinking will be hard to cultivate, and you will meet a lot of resistance. But independent thinking is super important for creating the best version of yourself. We have to walk alone if we want to go live a life that is above the mediocre. People will go after you and criticize you when you put yourself out there, but that is part of the climb.

Superhero

Joe Rogan always talks about the idea of being "the hero in your own movie".With that in mind ask yourself what will your hero do in this situation? Joseph Campbell also refers to similar ideas of heroes and ideals in his work. These types of archetypes are very powerful in keeping us motivated and moving us forward. In modern culture, we have forgotten to look at our past to find strength.

Warriors are not just people in the military or law enforcement. We are all warriors in a spiritual sense. We have to fight daily battles in our lives. At work in the boardroom, office, and all other areas of life.

Creating a superhero version of yourself might sound weird, but it's a great way to start getting momentum. Going after this superhero ideal will elevate your life to the next level. In Asian cultures, this has been used for a very long time by warrior traditions to build confidence and strength.

(5)Dream big because what is the alternative?

If we don't dream big then what else do we have? Do we just settle? Do we just go for the socially acceptable or mediocre? No!! We have a responsibility to go after what we want. Because when you are 80 years old, you will have to look yourself in the mirror and admit that you did not go for it.

2

What Is Self Discipline ?

Let's start at the dictionary definition of Self Discipline:

"The ability to control one's feelings and overcome one's weaknesses; the ability to pursue what one thinks is right despite temptations to give up and stop."

This, in a nutshell, is Self-Discipline. However, the attainment of self-discipline is challenging. Most people live without any form of discipline and the price they pay for that is unknown to them. They prefer not the pay the price of Self Discipline to live a successful and fulfilling life. Like they say "Ignorance is bliss".

Like I mentioned in the introduction of this book Self Discipline is slightly different from normal discipline. Normal discipline in the conventional military or rules in society has one thing in common. It has the threat of external force or punishment. However, Self-discipline is different.

Self Discipline is where external threats are no longer the motivating factor for following rules. The person applying Self-discipline becomes the authority over himself. He has made the choice to take control over his own life and ultimately his destiny. This is why elite special operations soldiers and elite athletes use Self-Discipline. They know the immense power they get through self-discipline.

Self Control

In order for you to become Self-Disciplined, you need to cultivate the ability to do the right thing on the right time whether you feel like or not. Your biggest obstacle to this goal will be Instant gratification.

Instant Gratification

Instant gratification is something that plagues the majority of people on this planet. We are all guilty of it sometimes, however Self-Disciplined individuals very rarely break their code and give in to the temptation.

What is Instant Gratification?

Instant gratification is the desire to experience pleasure right now and without any delay. You want something right now and that is it. Examples of instant gratification are parties, gossip, shopping, alcohol, drugs, smoking, sugar, fast food, social media likes and comments etc.

Delaying Gratification

Delaying gratification is the opposite. When you delay gratification, you have long term goals. You think long term to reach your objectives. You act accordingly and don't compromise to achieve your goals. You reject instant gratification for something much bigger. Your success is your only focus.

The key to all Self Discipline is delaying gratification. That means fighting all your natural impulses. Your brain is designed to keep you comfortable and help you survive. It does not care for your happiness. It has no regard for your goals and your self-discipline comes in the way of its impulse to get what it wants right now.

The Triune Brain Theory

The neuroscientist Paul D. MacLean created the Triune Brain Theory. In this theory, Maclean states that the human brain is actually 3 brains in one, hence the name "triune brain."

Let's take a look at the 3 brains MacLean refers to:

(1) The Reptilian brain

This is the oldest and most ancient part of the human brain. This part is very similar to the brains of lizards. This part of the brain has primitive processes like feeding, sex, exploration, dominance, and aggression. You will find this part of the brain at the brainstem and the cerebellum.

(2)Mammalian brain

MacLean states that after a very very long time a second brain evolved called the mammalian brain. This brain evolved over the first one and is today referred to as the limbic system.

"The old-mammalian brain, or the limbic system, adds behavioral and psychological resolution to all of the emotions and specifically mediates the social emotions such as separation distress/social bonding, playfulness, and maternal nurturance." (Jaak Panksepp in Affective Neuroscience: The Foundations of Human and Animal Emotions (1998).

The limbic system according to the scientist Panksepp also controls "subjective feelings and emotional responses."

Modern business and especially tech business has exploited the limbic system for massive profits. Think about all the social media platforms out there today. They are designed to exploit and reflect all the dominant human emotions.

Recently the entrepreneur and tech genius Elon Musk went on the Joe Rogan podcast. On the show, he said that the most successful social media platforms are the ones that resonate most with our Mammalian brain(limbic system)He goes on to say that these social media systems, represent an increasing share of society's total intelligence. Musk ended the topic saying this: "Imagine all those things, the sort of primal drives, there's all the things that we like and hate and fear, they're all there on the internet. They're a projection of our limbic system."

This is the reason why people get addicted to social media. People waste hours and hours of their lives on these platforms. They feel like they have no control over it.

(3)Neomammalian brain (Human Brain)

The Neomammalian brain or the human brain is the last part of the brain to develop. To put in simple terms the Neomammalian brain has to do with our logical and reasoning abilities. This is a uniquely human ability.

Humans Are Not Rational Most Of The Time

There is a perception with a lot of people that humans are very logical. Yes, we have moments of logic, but 90% of what we do is coming from the more ancient part of our brain and is anything but logical. We get dominated by the older and more primitive parts of the brain. This is the reason why it seems there is always a lot of chaos around the world. That is because there is. Sure we have made a lot of progress along the way, but we still struggle to keep it all together.

Conflict

We are in conflict with ourselves. Mainly because we are unaware of the massive power our brains have over our actions. Also, we do not know that we can do something about it and create better lives for ourselves. So this brain of ours is complex, and we need to keep an eye on it.

The problem with so many people letting their minds run free is that we now have so many social problems. These issues traced back to people just being out of touch with the reality of their own minds. Another way of looking at it is like the movie The Matrix where people are stuck in an artificial reality, and they are not aware of it.

The people who are stuck in the matrix are the people who are the followers in society. They don't question anything and have lost the ability to think critically. They are under total control of their minds. They have no mental self-discipline.

Most modern societies have created a culture where we have lost touch with who we really are. In the western world especially people have started to evaluate human problems as these little things in crystal boxes that we need to medicate, assess and label as modern human problems.This process of modern human culture is the problem.We have started to evaluate ourselves as these supposedly rational beings that do things just because of the situation we are in. We have totally forgotten about the animal inside ourselves. We are not like monkeys, we are monkeys.We are a very advanced species of primate that has a very complex brain. This brain and body have very ancient parts that humans tend to forget when we talk about problems in our lives or in society.

This Is The Challenge Of Self Discipline

The reason I gave this particular description of the 3 brain theory is to give you and an understanding of the ancient forces you are struggling against. This is the reason why success is so hard. It's hard to consistently fight these very powerful forces. And if someone does not implement Self Discipline into their lives then success will stay a dream only. Self Discipline needs to be something that is a way of life.

Delaying Gratification is one of the biggest challenges for us. Instant gratification plagues most people on this planet. Most people want to get what they want right now. They want it now, and they want it without any concern for the long-term consequences. They allow those ancient parts of their brains like the limbic system to dominate them.

There is a constant battle going on every day of your life. This battle is doing what is right vs. what is nice, easy, fun and pleasurable.

Biology Is Ruthless

Earlier in this chapter, I gave a general explanation of the 3 brain theory and how complex human biology is. One thing that humans don't contemplate a lot is how ruthless biology as a whole is. This planet is one giant organism. Humans live here with other animals and plants. As a whole, we make up this giant melting pot of life. Earth itself is part of the universe. We are influenced by the sun, moon and everything else around us. We as humans have a very limited understanding of how things really work.

My point with all this is that you should always keep in mind how ruthless and brutal biology is. Like I mentioned before ,your goals, feelings, success, and life means nothing to it. Biology just steams forward like a machine. It's your responsibility to resist the forces that create havoc on your mind and body.

How Do We Resist It?

To resist our own biology and the biology of this planet we need to embrace self-discipline and take control of our natural impulses. But there is another key component that might seem unrelated to Self-Discipline. You need to constantly be learning. You should be reading books about human psychology, biology, and evolution, I get it you can't read everything but study the basics so you understand yourself and the world you live in better. This will give you a great insight into how Self-Discipline keeps everything together. You have to develop as a human.

Fighting That Voice(Impulses)

We live in magnificent ancient bodies. These bodies have brains that react to impulses. If you want to become Self Disciplined you need to recognize these impulses and resist them.

The payoff you will get for building Self Discipline is massive. If you do this right your life will change.

3

Your Friendship With Pain

Pain will be something you will have to confront. Most humans run when they are confronted by pain. Whenever you take positive actions like going to the gym, quit smoking, writing that report, eating healthy or getting up early, you might feel pain. You will feel discomfort. Your first thought will be to stop. This is where most people end their effort with Self-Discipline.

They start feeling discomfort and they give up. They feel pain the first time and immediately stop. They want to go back to comfort now. Instant gratification is what they want. They can't take the pain a bit longer to get the results they want. So they give up and run to comfort.

These shadows in our minds are scary for most humans. When they go into these territories in their minds for the first time they resist it, they turn around and run.

What you need to do is turn around and confront the pain. Make friends with it. When you start feeling discomfort smile at it and own it. Tell yourself that it's fine to feel pain or discomfort. Once you feel the pain realize that this is your signal that you are doing the right thing. Walk through the darkness. Start loving these experiences because you know they are making you stronger.

People Don't Like Change

The obvious thing about self-discipline is that you need to change. But there is another thing that plagues humans. This is the fact that Humans hate change.

Most people will never change. Especially in today's comfortable environment where people get anything they want with the press of a button. They get seduced by modern comfort. So they delay change and improvement.

That is why things like new years resolutions never work. People are too comfortable and they want instant gratification. So most people never change. But like I mentioned in the previous chapter biology is ruthless. Life goes on and before you know it all kinds of chaos have broken out.

For example, a person starts to get overweight and thinks about losing some weight by starting a new workout plan. So the person tells himself he will start in 3 weeks when the new year starts. So the new year starts and nothing happens. He thought about change for a few minutes but then got seduced by the comfort and that doughnut on the table. He didn't listen to his friend who told him to be disciplined and start exercising and eating healthy.

So what happens? Biology strikes hard and ruthlessly. A year later he becomes seriously ill and the doctor says he is a diabetic. Something he could have prevented if he had self-discipline and took control of his life.

So yes biology waits for nobody. But in today's environment, there is another enemy that is allowed to seduce and comfort the masses of people out there. This enemy is feelings. The modern world is addicted to feelings.

They have given their feelings absolute priority over everything else. If someone feels sad, angry, depressed, and bad then the world has to stop and comfort that person. The world has been seduced by this addiction to feelings.

They have traded the truth for comfort. They won't point out problems, they will hide behind feelings. When a person can't walk up the stairs they will not say you are fat. They will say, "He is just a little tired".

When a person failed his test they won't say "You are lazy", they will say "He had a bad day".

When someone is late they won't point out the bad manners they will just say "That's OK".

We hide from the truth so we can feel comfy and coddled. In most developed countries like the US, Canada, and Europe people live in coddled spoilt societies. The results of this are that society as a whole is becoming weaker and weaker. Today's society gives each other hugs for everything. But unfortunately what many people need is slap in the face to wake up from the trance they are in.

This leads to people really struggling on an individual level to change when they have to. This also makes people give up very easily when they decide they want to change. They are mentally weak.

We mentioned the importance of accepting pain earlier in this chapter. The problem is that in today's world pain is avoided at all costs. The brutal reality of biology is that the clock is ticking and your time is running out. Every second you allow yourself to get seduced by emotion, warm hugs, participation trophies and modern comforts you are getting deeper into trouble.

Here is another newsflash. If you don't make the changes necessary to live your best life you will probably live a life of depression, unhappiness, and stress. This is just how biology rips comfort to pieces. Again, biology has no feelings whatsoever and if you don't get on the same playing field by adapting Self-Discipline you will lose. And lose badly.

Let me use an analogy to explain how it goes in life for most people. Let's imagine every person on this planet is on a ship on the ocean. This ship represents your life. This ship is made up of your life story. This ship includes everything. The way you live, what you eat, your lifestyle and self-discipline or the lack of self-discipline.

Now let's imagine everyone wants to go North because North is where success is. The problem is that most people that have no Self- Discipline in their lives think they are going North but they are actually heading South. South is where the rocks are. The rocks mean danger and death. Most people end up on the rocks.

So what happens when people hit the rocks? They freak out and act surprised. They don't know what happened. They don't understand how everything around them turned into chaos. Then they start remembering the new year's resolutions they didn't follow through on. They remember the time spent partying when they should have been studying. They remember all those doughnuts and ice cream they ate when should have been eating healthy. But now its too late.

Don't be one of those people who is going in the wrong direction. You need to realize the seriousness of the situation and make the changes necessary so you can go North.

What To Do If You Are On The Rocks Now?

If you are on the rocks now then I have some good news and some bad news. The good news is that you can still make it north. The bad news is you will have to not only accept pain as a friend, but you will also have to make it your brother. You will need to look for the pain. You will need to embrace pain so that you become so strong that the natural momentum of your efforts pushes you north.

The Bottom Line Of Self Discipline

You need to learn to do things you hate. The world we live in today tells us to just be comfortable and that we should avoid things we don't like. This is the biggest reason why so many people don't get what they want in life. To get what you want you to need to accept the following point: You have to start doing things you don't like doing. In fact, you need to become excellent at those things that you don't like doing.

A lot of people walk around saying that "I just want to follow my heart or my passion".Listen, that whole idea was built in a dream world. In reality, even the people that do things they love for a living sometimes have to do things they hate.

Talk to the most successful people on the planet and they will tell you the same thing. Sure I agree, find the thing you love, but to get there you might have to walk through a lot of crap. And guess what? Once you achieve the thing you want you still need to do some things you hate. This is the real world.

A lot of people quit their jobs and start their own businesses and then get a rude awakening. They thought now that they work for themselves they only get to do things they love. Unfortunately, the world of business doesn't work that way. Anything of value on this planet takes discipline and hard work to turn into reality.

This way of thinking is unfortunately widespread in the world we live in. It's especially prevalent in the online world of business and social media. The internet has created a massive opportunity for many people to create a living online and this has created the false idea of overnight success.

The whole modern entertainment industry including social media and others has created the false reality of overnight success. People buy into this idea of becoming rich and famous overnight. They see the post on social media showing someone posing in a car full of cash. The guy in the car says he became rich in a month and you can do the same. People buy into this rubbish.

Unfortunately, we now have a culture of entitlement. People want all their dreams to come true right now. They don't want to hear about things like hard work, perseverance. patience and self-discipline. They want the magic pill, the quick fix so that they can get that warm fussy feeling inside. The last thing they want is to do things they hate to get what they want. All they want is the big check and the pictures on social media.

You see it everywhere. In business, people start online and the first thing they ask is how they can outsource most of the work. I have nothing against delegating and outsourcing. However, that should not be your first priority. In fact, you need to do the hard work yourself first to get a better understanding of how your business works and what your employees go through. You need to do the hard work first before you earn the right to start playing the big boss man.

In fitness, people see their favorite movie star on TV and they think I want to look like that guy. The first thing they start looking for is some kind of supplement or protein powder that will build them that physique. They don't start with a workout and start doing the hard work necessary to get that body. In my own life, I hate running but I still do it because it gets me where I want to go in terms of my fitness and health goals. The upside of running totally outweighs the downside of my feelings towards running.

With dating and relationships, it's the same. A guy sees a beautiful woman somewhere and he asks his coworker to go ask the girl for her phone number. He doesn't have the courage to get into the "uncomfortable" situation and go talk to the girl. He wants all the upside with no downside.

Self-Discipline will teach you how to shut out all these voices in your head trying to stop you from success. Your discipline will keep you in check when you don't want to do the hard work necessary to get to where you want to go. It's now up to you to do the hard work to build a culture of Self Discipline in your life.

4

The Culture Of Cause And Effect

Talking about self-discipline is the easy part. Implementing Self-Discipline is the hardest part. Many people think that the daily actions of Self- Discipline are the hardest part. That is not the case. Although daily Self-Discipline is challenging it's not the hard part. Implementing and building a culture of discipline in your life is the hard part. Creating rules for your life with a foundation of Self-Discipline is the hard part.

Once you have achieved the foundation and start living your code then Self-Discipline becomes a lot easier. Self-discipline structure will give you security and confidence. You will learn that once you become a Self-Disciplined individual that living by this code will become very important to you. It will become your new normal and something you will learn to take pride in.

Developing Self Discipline

You can't just have discipline in one area of life. It doesn't work that way and it's not effective. Slack off in one area and it influences all other areas of life.

Foundations

Cause and Effect

Before we start this chapter I want to make one point abundantly clear. The whole universe functions on a very important principle. This principle is called cause and effect. This means everything you do has an effect. Every action you take will lead to something else. Whether that something else is positive or negative is up to you. It's up to the choices you make every day. The sum total of those choices will lead to either success or failure in whatever you are doing in life. Everything you do matters.

The Culture of Self Discipline

The biggest mistake people make is dabbling in Self-Discipline. They think just doing one thing differently will get them what they want. They think they want Self-Discipline so they make a change in one area of their lives and think that is going to get them what they want. For example, they want to lose weight and think by just eating well and exercising they will reach their goals.

People think they want to try out self-discipline. So they think "I'm going to give it a week and see if it works" or "Let's try it for a month".They put one foot in the water but don't commit. Here is the reality: If you don't jump in the water and submerge yourself in a culture of Self-Discipline then you have already lost. You are done. Most people fail because they dabble in Self-Discipline. But there is a more important thing that they miss. The thing they don't do that makes all the difference is that they don't make a commitment.

27

You Need To Make a Commitment

I see this all the time with guys who want to improve their lives. They want to get better but they hold back. They don't commit. They think if they "give it a go" they can tell everyone they gave it their best shot and it didn't work out. They think just trying will get them there.

There is a famous story of a Karate Master in Japan. In the story the master sees a student struggling to execute a move in class. The Master asked him what the problem is. The student answers and says, "I'm trying".The master looks at him and says, "Stop trying, just do it".This is the mindset most people have. They are "just trying" and at a subconscious level, they believe they can't do it. This subconscious belief holds them back from success. So they keep on "trying" and never just step up and do it.

Most people have a mental block or a disadvantage before they even begin. They have already decided they are lost. They have already decided on an unconscious level they can't do it. So they go in with a halfhearted effort so they can tell people and themselves that they "tried".

In the modern world, we lost this little thing called "faith" or "belief".You need to have faith in yourself that you will not just try Self Discipline but you will do it. Believe it and make a commitment to building a culture of Self Discipline and with that a culture of success. But you have to make a decision that that is the way that it's going to be.

Many people will hear me say this and say: "Ahh good talk but it's not that easy".Well yes, it's not easy, but nothing of any value is easy to get. Change the way you think about this and change your life. Make a decision today that you will become successful no matter what it takes. Self-Discipline will be the vehicle to get you there.

Everything in your life needs to change to make a massive transformation. If you want big results commit and go all in. If you want to get what you have never had before then you need to do what you have never done before.

5

The Mind

(1)The Mind

The mind is complex and is a place that creates your reality. The mind like mentioned earlier in this book is influenced by ancient and newer parts of the brain.

Emotions

Another major factor is emotions. Emotions are some of the most powerful forces in the universe. If you allow your emotions to control your mind, you will struggle to have a successful life. If you learn how to get control of your emotions you will feel that you gain more confidence and power in your life.

We live in a world addicted to emotions. People allow emotional addiction to dictate their choices and control their lives. You can just spend a few minutes on social media to see that. Better yet, put on the news for a few minutes, and you will see the emotional addiction everywhere.

The puppet masters of big corporations and governments have known for a long time that emotions have the power to control societies. They know that by creating certain emotions in society, they can reach certain objectives. They also know most people will blindly follow their emotions without question. This is why people will spend hours arguing on social media comments. They let their anger take control of them and then waste hours arguing with a stranger they never met before.

The reality is that it's natural to feel emotions. However, the question is how do you react to them?

There are ways to manage your emotions, for example, breathing techniques. The special operations forces are masters at getting control over emotions. Their lives are lived in a pressure cooker environment. If they don't learn to manage their emotions effectively, they can lose their lives.

The problem for soldiers is not just the short term threat of death but also long term negative effects. The negative effects are depression, anxiety, trouble sleeping, irritability, heavy drinking, or other symptoms of mental and physical stress.

Let's take a look at some ways you can manage your mind and emotions more effectively:

Breathing

Breathing can be a powerful tool to instantly get control over emotions like fear and anxiety. It's a very powerful technique that special operations units use, and it's called Box Breathing. Box breathing is a technique that uses deep breathing to calm down the heart rate and focus the mind.

It works like this:

-Start by trying to get into a relaxing position.Sit down if possible. If you can't sit, then stand where you are and close your eyes.
   -Sit up straight and focus.
   -Breath out to clear your lungs. You want to get rid of all the oxygen in your lungs
   -Start by inhaling deeply and slowly through your nose. Do this slowly to the count of four.
   -Focus now on holding this breath for another quiet count of four.
   -Exhale through your mouth. Again this happens to the quiet slow count of four.
   -Then wait for a slow count of four and repeat.
   -You can do this exercise for a few minutes until you start feeling relaxed.

Meditation

If I can take one tool with me to a new reality, it would be meditation. Meditation is a superpower that is available to all of us for free. All you have to do is practice it and make it a habit. Sounds easy right? Well, yes and no. If you can get yourself to do it, it becomes easy. The benefits are endless, and the quality of your life will improve.

There are many different opinions about meditation. Many people think that meditation is only done by monks. They also think that it's connected to only Buddhism or Hinduism. The truth is that meditation is open to anybody to use as a tool for self-improvement. It can be a secular or religious experience. You can give it whatever meaning you want, it does not matter. The benefits you get will still be the same.

There are many different ways or methods to meditate. The choice is up to you. My primary method of meditation is a type of guided meditation by Centerpointe. This technology has done wonders for my mental health and it's something that I recommend for anyone and especially for people that think meditation is hard or not something they think they can master. CenterPointe Holosync meditation simplifies the process and puts you in a meditative state a lot easier than conventional meditation. Again I have to emphasize that getting yourself to do it regularly and following instructions are the important parts.

Zazen

Twice a week, I do a form of Zen mediation called Zazen. There are many forms of Zen meditation, but this is very simple. The meditation is done by sitting down and focusing on your breath. By doing this practice, you will gradually start feeling the calming effects and go into a deeper meditative state. If you are a martial artist, then you probably use similar breathing in your practice and it should come naturally when you meditate. If you are not a martial artist, then dont worry, it's a simple process to learn. However, to get the full positive effects, you need to be consistent in your practice.

You can practice in the following way:

-Sit on the ground with your legs crossed. I recommend sitting on a desk chair with a straight back for beginners. This will help you focus on your breath if you are a beginner. Sitting on the floor distract beginners and scare people with injuries from mediation. So just start with a chair and if you want to move to the ground a few months later, then do it.

-Try and sit upright and balanced. Posture is very important. Don't lean in any direction, sit up straight.

-Close your eyes or keep it open if you want. But I find it easier to stay focused with my eyes closed.

-Breathing is the key to this meditation. Start by taking a long slow breath in. Try to go for about 90% in. (Don't try to go as full as possible)

-With the out-breath, go out slow and breath out 100%

-Repeat this process and build up a rhythm with this type of breathing. Just keep your focus on your breath.

-Remember to especially focus on that out-breath and keeping it long and deliberate.

-In Zen, they say the breath in meditation is similar to the roar of a tiger.

The mind is open to all kinds of suggestions, consciously and unconsciously. It's easy for the mind to get overwhelmed and cluttered. When the mind gets overwhelmed and cluttered, it easily gives in to instant gratification and the resistance of pain. In order to strengthen the mind, you need to implement some type of meditation into your life. It doesn't have to be long, but 20-30 minutes a day is a must to clear your mind and spend some time with yourself and focus on what is important. This is the time where you get rid of all the garbage running around your mind and you get yourself back to neutral.

Don't look for instant results with meditation. This is not a quick fix. The results of meditation are subtle, but you will start noticing changes after a few months of consistent practice. You will find yourself calmer, more focused and in control.

Spiritual

The modern world and especially the scientific world, has been very harsh towards the religious and spiritual. Science has made vast generalizations about all spirituality and has been calling for an end to it all. This culture has grown and the importance of having a spiritual life has decreased rapidly. Interestingly enough in the countries where spirituality and religion have disappeared, things like depression and unhappiness have increased.

I'm not here to encourage any specific religion or spirituality. However, I am saying that there is value in a spiritual life, and whatever elements or form you choose to adopt or make your own is your choice. Religion and spirituality have been with a man since the beginning of time. An internal world of stories, myths, and meaning give humans direction and stability. You don't need to believe in God or the afterlife to get value from spiritual life. But if you choose to believe in that, then go for it.

The great warrior traditions have relied on religion to give them strength, hope, and courage in times of adversity. The Samurai in Japan adopted Buddhism after witnessing the extreme courage and bravery of Zen Buddhist Monks. The Samurai witnessed monks fighting and dying with no fear of death. This impressed and intrigued the Samurai.

They learned that through studying Zen and Mediation, they became better warriors and had a better life. Even modern warriors pray to the universe, the force or God when they go into battle. Rationality alone is not always enough in times of extreme chaos and adversity. In times of overwhelming stress, men start breaking, and then they rely on their spiritual world to share the burden. This burden-sharing through meditation or prayer often makes the difference between winning or losing. Between life or death.

In modern Psychology, a similar theory exists. They call it responsibility transfer. By believing in a higher force or power give men courage and self-belief. Men start performing above and beyond their capabilities. These powers get elevated through spirituality. Like I mentioned before, whether it's real or not is irrelevant. The results speak for itself.

Visualization

Another layer on top of meditation is visualization. Visualization is something that's also been used for thousands of years and is related to meditation but is slightly different. These days visualization is used by many successful sports teams and business professionals to get what they want out of life.

There is a famous story about how Micheal Phelps used visualization in his preparation for the Beijing Olympics, and this helped him to go on and win many gold medals. You can read more about it in the famous book "The Power of Habit" by Charles Duhigg.

Phelps had a brilliant coach that taught him how to master his mind. Specifically, he taught him how to visualize. The coach called it "the videotape". He would instruct Phelps to go home and watch "the videotape" after training. The "videotape" was a visualization process where Phelps would visualize the perfect race. Every morning before he got out of bed and every night before sleep, he would lie in bed watching "the videotape". He would visualize jumping off the blocks and then in slow motion, see himself executing the perfect race. He would experience the race in detail. He would feel the water on his skin and how he would rip off his goggles at the end. He would know everything about the race in his mind.

Before swimming practice, his coach would tell him to put in "the videotape". Then he would swim amazing times and keep improving. Sometimes Phelps would change the videotape by imagining things going wrong in a race but still swimming a perfect race. He would visualize how he would overcome problems if they come up in a race. For example, he trained in the dark to prepare for losing his vision in a race. He would then visualize that happening in his "videotape" and still win his race.

Combined with the visualization process was a set of core habits that Phelps would use every day. For example, stretching, eating the same food, listing to the same music, etc. When he visualized, he incorporated these habits. Everything became a smooth operating machine

On Aug. 13, 2008, Phelps started his routine in Beijing. It was a big day at the Olympics and Phelps had already turned on "the videotape".The process has already started. By the time he hit the water, he was already 80% finished with his tape. The swim was just finishing the process. That morning as soon as he hit the water, his goggles started filling with water. By the final turn, he could not see anything. He was swimming with no vision. Most other people would have started panicking and lost the race. For Phelps, it was another "videotape" that he has watched hundreds of times. He still went on to win gold. This is a simple version of the story but it illustrates the enormous power of visualization.I recommend reading the amazing book by Charles Duhigg.,"The Power Of Habit", to learn more about habits and routines and how you can combine it with visualization.

Habits

By creating strong positive habits in your life, you will make it easier for your brain to get into line in terms of what you want to achieve. In the previous part of this chapter, I talked about visualization and how Phelps used it t reach high levels of success. I also touched on the topic of habits.

The habits that Phelps used in combination with visualization is called Keystone Habits. The keystone habits are what the author Charles Duhigg refers to as habits that have the power to transform your life.

Here are Examples of powerful keystone habits :

- Make your bed every morning
- Having Daily routines
- Exercising Every Day
- Planning Your Days and Weeks

Digital Declutter

The mind has never in history been exposed to so many outside stimuli. The mind has never been fed a constant stream of information like it is now. The digital and information revolution has been both a blessing and a curse. The modern tools we use, like smartphones and computers, are very powerful. These tools can make our lives better but can also do a lot of damage. It might be hard to spend less time on your phone. But you need a digital declutter. Schedule one day a week away from your smartphone. If you are in a position where your job requires you to always be in contact with the outside world then get a cheap dumb phone that only takes calls for emergencies. Being online 24 hours a day is not good for you.

The Big Sponge

The mind is a big sponge, and it sucks up all the information it gets. It analyzes the information without judgment. So for example, if you watch soap dramas all day long, five days a week, then this will start dominating your mind. It will influence you whether you are aware of it or not. It's the same for the opposite scenario. If you focus on reading a good book every day, then those thoughts will start dominating your mind.

This is similar in all areas of life. Like the people we surround ourselves with, the music we listen to, the movies we watch, the websites we visit and everything else we do consistently. Like I said before, the mind does not judge. The mind just takes the dominant information and tries to create a reality based on that. This represents one form of mind programming.

The other form of mind programming is childhood programming. The things we got exposed to since birth.The things our parents did or said. The teachers, churches, and other "role models" we had, and the schools we attended. Our formative years as babies and young children played a massive part in our brain development. A lot of fears, phobias, and mental patterns can be traced back to this part of our lives, and we have been running these mind programs for a long time.

We can take a look at a lot of issues or problems in our own lives. By looking closer, we will see many patterns or things that we did as children that we are still doing today. In my life, there were a few patterns I was running since I was a child into my twenties. I did not even realize I was doing it because I was not aware of my mental habits. For example, the way I was speaking to my friends. Sometimes I would be rude for no reason. I had to take a step back, recognize this behavior and change it. This is just a simple example of a bad mental habit that many of us carry with us. Another example could be reacting in a negative way when something bad happens in our lives. We can recognize this mental habit and decide to react differently next time we are in a similar situation.

The good news is we can reprogram our minds over time. It will not be easy, but with consistent practice, we can make massive improvements in the way our minds operate. And by doing this we can make huge improvements in the quality of our lives.

Change Your Mindset

Everything starts with your mindset. Carol Dweck wrote the fantastic book Mindset: The New Psychology of Success. In the book, she talks about the fixed mindset and the growth mindset. We have to remember that things don't have to be the way they currently are. We can learn, change and improve. Things are not set in stone. You are not who you think you are. We can all change and become better at living. It's a choice!

People with a fixed mindset will probably not read this book since they think it's pointless. People with a fixed mindset think that life is the way it is, and you can't change it. However, people with a growth mindset think you have the potential to become whoever you want to be if you put in the work and stay focused.

The mindset you create for yourself is important. This mindset will be the way you think and approach life. Your mindset will make or break your success.

Mindset Guidelines

The following is the mindset of a driven, successful man:

1- He Accepts responsibility for everything in his life, this includes the good and the bad.

He believes that he does not owe anyone what he would be in the future, or what he has already become. He accepts that he is responsible for his own actions because he has the awareness that everything that happens to him comes out of his free will.

To be the man that you want to become means having the power to change what you can and accept the things that you cannot, without blaming other people for untoward consequences of your actions. Responsibility for your own life means that you are capable of making your own choices. That also means that you understand that being the ultimate man does not mean that you have achieved perfection – you would still experience good and bad situations, and you should be man enough to accept that they are part of your life.

Remember that you are no longer a child. Should you encounter hardships, do not think that you should have listened to what other people said – you are a grown man capable of making your own mind. There is no one else that drove you to a bad situation apart from yourself. If you find yourself taking advantage of a good opportunity, then you also owe it to yourself. No one is responsible for your own defeats and successes. You have the sole ownership to what you can make in your life, whether it is good or bad. Starting today, think that you are a person capable of thinking for yourself without having the need for other people to make decisions. There is no choice but to accept responsibility for your own self.

2- Find your purpose and pursue it with everything that you have.

If you feel that you are driven to act and improve yourself to chase after your goals, then you have this Alpha trait. If you are aware that no one should be able to stop you from getting the things that you want as long as you keep focused, then you know that there is no way you can fail in anything that you strive to do.

Without a sense of purpose, you would be swayed from one direction to another. You would not be able to be half the man that you think you should be. If you don't know your purpose, then lock yourself in a room until you find out what your purpose is.Do whatever it takes to figure out what your purpose is.

3- He is prepared to walk alone when he goes after his purpose.

He knows that he will be criticized and opposed, and these challenges excite him. When you want to be a man that can surpass the standards of anyone that you know, you are aware that you are thinking unconventionally. That awareness that you are unlike most people should lead you into knowing that you will not be followed by everyone at the beginning. People will not buy the idea that you would succeed.But they would want to be with you once you are able to show them that you can make things work even on your own.

You need to be prepared for challenges from the very people that would admire you in the future. These people would be your worst critics and your worst enemies at the beginning, but wait for it – once you are able to prove that they are wrong, they would want to root for you in the end. For this reason, think of criticism as a very exciting challenge that would give you rewards. Once you commit to your purpose and be rewarded by your hard work, you would realize that people would desire to be around you.

4 - He has his own reality, and other people are guests in it. Live your life by your own rules.

If you want to reach the top, you have to have a powerful belief that the truth for you may not be the truth for others. However, you have a very high standard on what is acceptable for you. Even though you are aware that most people around you are fine with what is going on, you want to live in a culture of excellence. For that reason, you choose to live in your own reality.

While you may accommodate people in your life they need to understand that if they do not want to be part of your competitive world they are free to leave. A compromise that is designed to make you mediocre and subscribe to another person's beliefs is not an agreement that is worth your time. Remember that from now on, you are the ruler of your own life. You do not need other people's approval in choosing how you should act or making decisions for yourself.

At this point, you are embarking on an adventure that would allow you to be a king of your own realm – you are not forcing people to enter your reality, and there is no reason for them to have the right to take charge of how you should live your life. Remember that you are the only one who truly knows yourself. Only you can tell what you can do in the future.

5- He looks for discomfort and then overcomes it, he knows that this is where growth takes place.

You are aware that life is not perfect, and there may be temporary setbacks to your goals. However, no matter how uncomfortable life may become, you see every problem as an opportunity to grow.

Of course, no one wants to be in a difficult position. However, you need to see that you are going nowhere if you are unable to test your limits or if you are unable to leave anything that you do not like anymore. If you think that you are going to be rejected or that you would fail if you choose to switch careers, then you need to think if you are satisfied being an ordinary person in a position that you do not like. Surely, going after what you truly want is worth every risk. If you want to see to it that you would be able to truly achieve your goals, then you should not be afraid of a little risk in exchange for bigger rewards. You are not losing anything but your life's prison.

Once you make the decision to reach your top potential, you will have a better understanding that no man, fictional or not, has claimed that life is easy. In fact, the more you strive to move towards perfection, the more you would discover that there are difficulties that you may have not encountered in the past – the more you improve, the tougher the challenges would be. Take this realization to mean that you would no longer be bothered by small problems – the more you immerse yourself into things that cause you discomfort, the more resilient you become.

6- Self-improvement is a part of his life until he dies.

A man with a warrior mindset believes in the concept of Kaizen, the Japanese belief that all things in the world are capable of being endlessly improved.

While you may understand that there is no way that the world that you are in can be perfect, aiming for constant and consistent improvement grants you the ideal that every situation or object in your reality can become better. By embodying this principle, you would have the peace of mind that even though you fall behind and make mistakes, you are capable of being able to fix what is broken and even make them work to your advantage. Because you believe that all things can be improved, you will want to find how you can make use of the resources that are around you.

Because you believe that you would be a better version of yourself, you would put your progress into a test. You would stop relying on others and discipline yourself to achieve your goals no matter what. After all, you have the certainty that the things that you cannot do today are the things that you would be able to do in the near future.

At this point, you have the understanding that your aim is to continuously improve all aspects of your life, no matter how difficult it can be.

7- Self-Education is very important to him.

He reads a lot and listens to audio programs to learn about a wide variety of subjects like psychology, self-help, philosophy, history, and evolution. This process of learning continues forever.

Successful men will find a way to continue learning, within or outside the walls of the academy. This is a true trait of most corporate leaders in the world, which makes it a point to read at least 5 books in a month. That means that even though these men were able to reach the peak of their careers, they still make it a point to continue their education through reading. The reason is simple – the extra knowledge that they may gain today can become a very useful skill that they can use should they find themselves wanting to immerse in another field of interest.

8- He controls his Mind and Emotions.

He uses meditation, breathing, and physical movement to make sure he is in a constant state of positive energy. He does not allow negative emotions to dominate his mind. He recognizes that negativity is part of life, and then immediately gets rid of negative emotions. Depressed people stay in negative states, he never does because he deals with it. That is the difference, he does not live in negative states of mind; he recognizes it, and then deals with it and moves on to the positive state of mind.

The Successful man is capable of maintaining his composure no matter what his environment is. The reason why he makes it a point to have a sound mind and heart, no matter how challenging the circumstances are is simple – clouded minds make clouded judgments, which he would never want to make. He aims to make logical and fair judgments all the time because it is the only way for him to make decisions.

This is where the training to become Self Disciplined becomes hard – right now, it may seem impossible for you to get your emotions grounded during a difficult time. It is very hard to think right when you are under pressure. You think that because it is very uncomfortable to be on the spot, you need to make a decision right away even when you are still uncertain of what you should do. Don't rush yourself – clear your mind first and once you are able to become calm, consider all the options that are laid out in front of you.

9- He has a mindset of winning.

He always approaches life from the mindset that he has already won. He visualized his victories before it happens. This is his reality.

There is no way for any person to achieve success in an instant. However, there is a way to plan success by taking goals one piece at a time. An Alpha understands that while he cannot teleport right into the goal that he wants to reach, he can devise a roadmap to success that would allow him to reach his destination in the most efficient way possible.

To do this, you need to first believe that no matter how daunting your goal is, you would be able to still reach it. All you need to do is to think about how you are going to trim down a goal into small, more actionable targets and then take them one by one. Make sure that you are able to mark your progress as you go to feel motivated as you go along the way. Should you hit a roadblock to your progress, you can make minor revisions to your plan in order to find the right tactic to hit a particular goal.

10- He has a sense of humor in adversity.

The Elite British Royal Marines Commandos has a principle that every Marine Commando has to learn. The rule is "Cheerfulness in the face of adversity".The Royal Marines Commandos know that reframing adversity in their minds and seeing the funny side of the whole situation gives them a mental edge. It creates powerful positive energy that pushes them through any level of adversity.

The successful man realizes that sometimes he should just laugh and see the funny side when things get tough. Difficult times often make a man feel down. However, a true man understands that when failure and disaster strikes, not everything is lost. He knows he can frame any situation in his mind so that he can see the funny side. He knows humor creates positive energy.

Looking at the funny side of things does great wonders. Not only do you avoid preventable stress, you also make use of your faculties to enable you to make better use of your time. By recognizing that you made a mistake and then quickly shrugging it off, your brain starts to process what you should have done and how you are going to make up for the mistake that you just committed. Having the ability to laugh at mistakes also allows you to regain your focus, which helps you quickly recover from a mishap.

11- He has Accepted death.

He does not hide from it and does not fear it. He thinks of it every day and this inspires him to live life to its fullest. He learned this from the ancient samurai tradition that thinks about death in the morning when they get up so they can get inspired to live a full and rich life every day.

Appreciating life and the opportunity to live for one more day inspires you to do what you can to improve yourself and the lives of people around you for the limited time that you have in this world. Once you have accepted that you would face death in a way that you do not expect, you would make it a point to live your life in ways that you never did in the past. It also makes you realize that there is so much that you still want to accomplish, and there is no better day to make dreams come true but today.

Once you adopt the principle of not fearing death, you would observe how much courage you gain – you become undaunted by the chance of failure, as long as you have measurable means to success. At the same time, you are motivated to improve and achieve as much as you can every day – you desire to learn more and start projects that you have shelved. Everything becomes important. Once you embrace the fact that you would possibly die tomorrow, you want each day to feel like you are about to leave a legacy behind.

12- He never complains.

Complaining is a waste of energy, especially if you are still in a position wherein you need to go back to work and fix an error. Complaining puts your motivation down, and once you think that there is nothing else that you can do about the situation and somebody else should be doing the fixing, then you are creating an even bigger problem than the situation itself. You are creating an infectious mindset that prevents people from thinking of solutions, and then induces a blaming marathon that would never end.

If you have the habit of complaining, ask yourself this question: is the task that you need to do so difficult that it exists outside your skillset? If you answer No to this question, then there is no reason to complain – just go ahead and do it already. Only incapable people whine.

13- He has incredibly high standards in life. He never compromises on these standards in all areas of life.

If you feel that you are never satisfied, then you already have the makings of being successful. Satisfaction becomes the end of curiosity and the start of making do with what exists around you. However, if you have the itch to continue improving all the details that you see in your reality for the benefit of everyone that belongs to your world, then you know that you have higher standards than everyone else.

Ordinary men will make do with what they have – they will be fine with the wage that an employer gives them, without even asking what they need to do to deserve a raise. They will be fine with the fact that there are other people that earn less than two dollars in a day, as long as they are content with the idea that they can pay rent. They are fine with the knowledge that less than a percent of the population actually owns all the industries in the world, and they are not part of that statistic.

If you are greatly disturbed by what is happening around you and you want to work for change, then that is a good thing. Because you feel annoyed or irritated with what is happening with the world, you are compelled to take action, compared to those that are simply saddened that injustice happens around them and they cannot do anything about it. When you have that itch for change, you would do whatever it takes to get that feeling out of your skin.

14- He sets massive goals and goes after them. He does not give up until he reaches his goals.

A successful man lives by the challenge of his goals – achieving goals and setting up personal challenges is both a habit and a hobby to him. Since Alphas are fond of discovering their current limits and how they can surpass them in the most efficient way possible, they also make it a point that they set massive goals. The more daunting they are, the better they sound.

Massive goals, no matter what they are, are still actionable as long as you can think of the best way to churn them down. Now, the churning down of these goals serves as an exciting hobby for an alpha – for example, he may see himself becoming the CEO of a very lucrative company, but he needs to lay out a roadmap made up of small, actionable, and timely goals to make this goal come true.

As he creates this plan, he is excited about taking all those steps as he thought it, and every time he succeeds, he becomes even more motivated to take the next one. Because he loves the feeling of being successful, he also becomes very excited in other large prospects that he has in mind. The achievement of massive goals gives him the power that he craves, and that is the knowledge that he can dictate what should happen to his life.

15- Fitness and health is one of his priorities.

He goes to the gym lift weights and does yoga for flexibility. He eats healthy and takes high-quality supplements to manage the demands of his lifestyle.

The secret to a great physique is simple: he considers his body and his mind as tools for success. For that reason, he sees to it that he gives his body the same attention that he does to his mind. He makes it a point that he is always in top shape to not only look presentable to other people but to also allow him to do more in a day.

Successful men consider fatigue as one of the enemies of achieving daily progress, and in order to eliminate that factor altogether, he makes it a point that he focuses on strengthening exercises. He also sees to it that he only eats healthy food that boosts his mind and body. He also does not get tempted with decadent food, alcohol, and illegal substances– he knows that to consume them is to make his body and mind less functional, thus delaying him in achieving his next target.

16- Self-Discipline.

Self- Discipline in life is his cornerstone. Discipline is reached by consistency in actions and not compromising on goals.

At the heart of every successful man is that unwavering discipline – he is a military unit on his own, and he believes that in order to win life battles, he needs to make sure that all his faculties are doing what is planned. Because he has his goals set in stone, there is no way that he could be tempted by the little devils of an ordinary man, like hitting the snooze button in the morning or having that extra shot of tequila when he has to wake up early.

Alphas know that in order to experience abundance, he has to figure out a way to avoid excess. He knows that before he takes control of other people and situations, he has to figure out how he can control himself.

6

The Body

Now that we covered the mind, it's time to move on to the body and everything that influences it. Although the body and mind are part of one big machine, we will discuss it as a separate part of who you are. The following components will make you perform at optimal levels:

Exercise

You have to implement physical exercise at least 5 days a week. You can take a break on weekends if you have to, but weekdays are non-negotiable. Personally, I do 6 days on and 1 day off. But if you are a beginner in this world of Self Discipline, then start with 5.

We are all busy people but we need to take time for physical training. This should be non-negotiable. I have listed 3 different types of physical training. There are many forms of exercise, however, in my opinion, these 3 gives you the most n return as an investment. For me there are no better forms of physical exercise than the following:

(1)Weight Training
  (2)Yoga
  (3)Running

(1)Weight Training

Weight training has to be the foundation for building a strong healthy body. Focus on traditional compound exercises. These are bench press, dead-lift, squats, and shoulder presses. Then add bodyweight exercises like pull-ups and push-ups and burpees.

Like I said before even if you are not a "gym person " then become one. Get over yourself and look at the big picture. The big picture is that weight training is the best way to build strength, build muscle, burn fat, boost testosterone and improve your overall health.

Sometimes weight training gets a bad rap from some health circles. However, the latest science concludes that the benefits of weight training are incredible and gives you the best bang for your buck. The latest studies also show that weight lifting is a superior option to cardio when it comes to burning fat and losing weight.

According to the MAYO Clinic you will get the following benefits from Weight training:

(1)Develop Stronger bones over time.

(2)Keep your weight in check

(3)Increase your Stamina

(4)Manage and Reduce the Symptoms of Chronic conditions

(5)Improve your focus and attention.

If I had to choose one form of exercise, then it would be weight training. Even if get forced to do only two exercises it would be dead-lifts and squats. With just those two exercises I would be able to stay healthy and strong

Vital hormones like testosterone that all males needs, get boosted when we lift weights and this is crucial when it comes to a man's health.With the environment changing and influencing our health we need our hormones to operate on an optimum level. Weight training is one of the ways that help us boost those hormones. But more on the importance of hormones later.

How do I get started with weight training?

The obvious part is to join a gym. However, the most important part is to have a plan and to stick with it.

Most people give up on training because they don't have a plan, so they get no results. Then they lose motivation and quit. Where to get a plan? Well, there are hundreds of good workout plans online to check out. Or check out my blog for some resources. You can get some workout plans for about $15- 20. It's worth it to spend some money on your body. It is an investment in yourself.

(2)Stretching/Yoga

I do Yoga twice a week to stretch out my body and keep me flexible and injury-free. It's also a great form of meditation.

Many guys won't even consider the idea of Yoga, but Yoga is one of the most valuable ways to improve your body and mind The benefits to your overall flexibility and strength are huge, not to mention the effect on your mind. It will help you deal with stress in a lot more efficient way.

Forget about Yoga classes where there is a hippie talking about the afterlife. There are many different types of yoga that will give you a kickass workout. As I said, the best classes are the ones where you get a good physical workout with a good teacher that is not full of crap.

If you are walking into a class and someone wants to cleanse your aura, walk out and find another school. There are many, and you can sit down and watch a class as an observer before you sign up for classes.

One of my favorite books on Yoga is written by a Navy SEAL, and I highly recommend you check it out. The book is called Kokoro Yoga by Mark Divine, and this book has all the tools to get you started and transform your life. One of the awesome parts of the book is the section on how to manage your breathing.

Benefits following a Yoga session:

Improves brain functioning.

Even for only twenty to thirty minutes of Hatha yoga can help enhance cognition and improve concentration as well as memory. This type of yoga is focused more on physical postures as compared to others which emphasize sequences or flow.

Decreases levels of stress.

According to a recent study conducted in the University of California, yoga has the capacity to reduce the action of proteins that are known to contribute in engendering inflammation.

Modifies gene expression.

A research study in Norway indicated that the numerous health benefits of this practice possibly come from its capability to modify gene expression in the body's immune cells.

Improves flexibility.

Bikram Yoga involves a total of 26 postures that are supposed to be accomplished within ninety minutes inside a heated venue. According to a study conducted by the Colorado State University, this kind of activity is associated to more flexibility in the lower back, shoulder, and hamstring. In addition, increased muscle strength and lesser body fat were observed.

Benefits following months of practice:

Decreases blood pressure.

Individuals who are hypertensive could benefit from yoga exercises. A study found that this activity is more effective in lowering blood pressure in comparison to those who engaged in other activities such as walking, counseling programs to lose weight, and nutrition.

Increases lung capacity.

Vital lung capacity increases after weeks of engaging in regular Hatha Yoga. Vital lung capacity which is a component of lung capacity refers to the greatest amount of air that may be expired after deep inspiration of air.

Enhances sexual function.

Yoga has demonstrated that it can increase a person's sexual desire and sexual satisfaction. Through yoga, women are able to familiarize themselves with their bodies and the extent of their capabilities.

Decreases chronic pain in the neck.

Iyengar Yoga emphasizes correct alignment and usage of supportive equipment during activity. Weeks of engaging in this exercise can help decrease intense pain among individuals suffering from chronic neck pain.

Alleviates chronic back pain.

Iyengar Yoga helps in enhancing mood and decreasing pain particularly with those who have difficulties with their lower back.

Help maintain blood sugar levels among diabetics.

Regular yoga practice can help in reducing weight and steadying levels of blood sugar.

Increases sense of balance.

The elderly or people over the age of 65 years usually experience problems with their sense of balance. With regular practice of yoga, this can be improved to avoid falls among elderly people.

Benefits following years of yoga practice:

Help develop stronger bones.

It is typical for the elderly to decrease bone density and bones becoming brittle. However, with yoga practice, they can improve their bone mineral density or gain bone.

Helps in reducing and maintaining an appropriate weight.

A research group from Seattle found a relation between regular yoga and reduced or properly maintained weight among thousands of healthy personalities. The overweight people who have regular exercise lost more or less five pounds at the time while those who are not gained.

Reduces risk of a heart ailment.

Yoga as one of the modifying changes people integrate into their lives may help in decreasing the risk of cardiac problems like high levels of cholesterol and sugar in the blood including hypertension.

Different Types of Yoga and Finding the Best One For You

Ashtanga Yoga.

A total of six sequences comprised of an array of postures usually instructed one position at a time. The majority of the sessions concentrate on what is referred to as the Primary Series. This is not so complicated for new participants but may be difficult for persons who have not started to exercise. Students learn in different phases, with the instructor helping out and teaching new poses while old ones are mastered.

Bikram Yoga.

This class involves accomplishing all 26 poses and 2 breathing exercises. Each one is held for one whole minute and is done two times. The class is held in a heated room and does not use music.

Hatha Yoga.

This is a slow and gentle type of yoga class that is well suited for beginners, people with mobility issues.

Iyengar Yoga.

This concentrates on the alignment of the body. Poses are meticulously instructed. Props like blankets, blocks, chairs, and straps may be used for the different poses. Each one is held longer as compared to other yoga classes. Classes are slowly paced and strict; however, students are assured to learn a lot. This fits well with any age, beginners, and people recuperating from any physical injury.

Power Yoga.

The classes are highly dynamic and sporty. It is a form of Ashtanga that turned western style. It started to use other various poses aside from those used in Ashtanga. This yoga activity has added moves that strengthen muscles particularly the core muscles. There are many poses accompanied by regulated breathing in between with lots of strength-building poses, pushups, and handstands. This is not suitable for individuals with limited mobility or injury and who would rather join in gentle yoga sessions.

Vinyasa Yoga.

This has a more rapid pace flow classes. They can cross over different schools of yoga and may move faster. This is great for individuals who easily get tired of the same routine they perform regularly.

Practicing Yoga At Home

Practicing yoga at home can save money, energy, and time. At the same time, no stranger or another person who will be looking at your behind as you execute the different poses required in class. A half hour of yoga at home is frequently more advantageous than driving yourself to a studio, searching for a spot to park, and others cashing in for every session you attend.

(3)Cardio

The biggest reason people fail with running is the lack of consistency and the absence of a plan.

Get Started

You've been hearing a lot of good things about running: how it has helped people lose a lot of weight, how it makes people feel good and accomplished, has lowered people's blood pressure, cholesterol levels, and so on. You want to try it out yourself, but you are not sure whether you are ready for it. You feel like you don't know where to begin.

If this is the feeling that you have right now, there's only one thing that you need to do: start shopping.

That's right. The first step to running is to shop for the right running shoes. Doesn't sound so hard, does it? If you already have running gear, buy an extra pair of socks. Signaling your mind that you are investing on something is a great motivator to get you started.

Follow a Beginner's Program

Now that you have your running shoes, you are probably really excited to get started. Nevertheless, there are few guidelines that you need to know first before you begin:

Start by walking. Running is an intense exercise, which means that you need to give your body time to adapt first. Walking will let your heart and muscles warm up and gradually increase. After putting your shoes on, start walking for about 30 minutes on flat terrain, then go home and reflect on how it made you feel. If it was effortless, then you are ready to kick it up a notch tomorrow.

The Beginner Runner's Schedule. Beginners are advised to go out there for 30 minutes a day, four days per week. This 30 minutes is not dedicated entirely to running; it can be a combination of running and walking.

Keep in mind that you will feel soreness and discomfort the following day after you run, which is why you need to start with walking first. In order to help you ease into the program, here is a running schedule meant for beginners (you will need a timer):

1st Week:

Day 1: Walk for 10 minutes. In the next 10 minutes, switch between running for 1 minute and walking for 1 minute. Spend the last 10 minutes walking.

Day 2: Walk for 10 minutes. In the next 15 minutes, switch between running for 1 minute and walking for 1 minute. Spend the last 5 minutes walking.

Day 3: Walk for 10 minutes. In the next 15 minutes, switch between running for 2 minutes and walking for 1 minute. Spend the last 5 minutes walking.

Day 4: Walk for 5 minutes. In the next 21 minutes, switch between running for 2 minutes and walking for 1 minute. Spend the last 4 minutes walking.

2nd Week:

Day 1: Walk for 5 minutes. In the next 20 minutes, switch between running for 3 minutes and walking for 1 minute. Spend the last 5 minutes walking.

Day 2: Walk for 5 minutes. In the next 21 minutes, switch between running for 5 minutes and walking for 2 minutes. Spend the last 4 minutes walking.

Day 3: Walk for 4 minutes. In the next 24 minutes, switch between running for 5 minutes and walking for 1 minute. Spend the last 2 minutes walking.

Day 4: Walk for 5 minutes. In the next 22 minutes, switch between running for 8 minutes and walking for 3 minute. Spend the last 3 minutes walking.

3rd Week:

Day 1: Walk for 5 minutes. Follow it with 10 minutes of running. Walk for 5 minutes after that. Run for another 5 minutes. Spend the last 5 minutes walking.

Day 2: Walk for 5 minutes. Follow it with 12 minutes of running. Walk for 5 minutes after that. Run for another 5 minutes. Spend the last 5 minutes walking.

Day 3: Walk for 10 minutes. Run for 15 minutes. Spend the last 5 minutes walking.

Day 4: Walk for 6 minutes. Run for 18 minutes. Spend the last 6 minutes walking.

4th Week:

Day 1: Walk for 5 minutes. Run for 20 minutes. Spend the last 5 minutes walking.

Day 2: Walk for 5 minutes. Run for 22 minutes. Spend the last 3 minutes walking.

Day 3: Walk for 3 minutes. Run for 25 minutes. Spend the last 2 minutes walking.

Day 4: Run for 30 minutes.

Stretching and Running Techniques

Most people think that running is just about putting one foot in front of the other really fast. However, there is more behind the science of running than that. Knowing the different running techniques will help improve your overall running experience and let you boost your speed, form and progress efficiently.

Always Stretch before you Run. Well-stretched muscles will ensure that you will have a great running workout because they will not be fatigued or sore afterwards. Not stretching can also lead to injury, which will further hinder you from doing your workouts regularly.

Here are the 10 steps on how to do a basic warm-up stretches. The entire routine will not take more than 5 minutes.

Step 1: Wall Push-ups

Base position: Stand three feet from the wall with feet in line with shoulders and flat on the floor. Place your hands against the walls with arms straight.

Lean hips forward, then bend knees slightly. Feel the stretch in your calf muscles. Repeat 3 times.

Next, resume base position. Bend your torso forward to waist height. Lift one foot forward with knee slightly bent. Lift the toes. Feel the stretch in the muscles under the calf. Repeat 3 times. Do the same for the other leg.

Resume base position. Put feet together and stand on your heels with arms straight to form a jackknife shape. Feel the stretch in your hips, shoulders and lower back. Repeat 3 times.

Step 2: Back Scratch

Hold your left elbow using your right hand and slowly push your elbow upwards and across the body until your left hand touches down your back, as if to scratch it. Slowly push your left elbow to bring the hand as far down as comfortable for you. Feel the stretch in your triceps and shoulders. Repeat 3 times and change arm.

Step 3: Hamstring Stretch

Lie flat on the floor. Bring your left leg straight up while keeping your right leg positioned with knee bent and foot flat on the floor. Loop an old towel over the arch of your left foot and slowly pull on it to push against the foot. Keep pulling until you feel the muscles in your leg contract. Repeat 3 times and change foot.

Step 4: Quadriceps Stretch

Kneel on the floor, but keep soles pointing upwards. While keeping your body straight and your arms to your side, lean back gradually and hold the position for 15 counts.

Step 5: Heel to Buttock Stretch

Stand on your left foot and keep yourself in balance by placing your right hand against a wall. Hold your right foot using your left hand and gradually lift the heel of your right foot to your buttocks. Keep your body straight throughout the process. Repeat 3 times and change foot. Feel the stretch in your quadriceps.

Step 6: Hip and Lower Back Stretch

Sit on the floor and cross your legs. Bring your right leg up and cross it over the left. Keep your left leg bent. Hug your right leg and bring it close to your chest. Twist your torso to look over your right shoulder. Hold for 8 seconds. Repeat with the other leg.

Step 7: Iliotibial Band Stretch

Lie down on your side and bring both legs bent as if in running position. Position lower leg toward the chest and position the upper leg back toward the buttocks as far as both legs can go. Hold for 30 counts before switching to the other side.

Step 8: Hamstring and Back Stretch

Lie down on your back and keep knees bent. Use your arms to bring your shins close to your chest. Hold for 30 counts.

Step 9: Bridge

Lie on your back with your feet flat on the floor. Bring your hips upwards to create a straight plane. Hold for 30 seconds and repeat 10 times. Feel the stretch in your quads and lower back.

Step 10: Groin Stretch

Sit on the ground with the soles of your feet placed together. Hold your ankles and keep your elbows on the inside of your knees. Slowly lean forward while gently pressing your knees to the ground. Push as low as what is comfortable for you. Hold for 15 counts.

The Right Pace

When you run, you think you will get out of breath. This is not true. In fact, if you huff and puff as you run, it means that you are going too fast. The right way to run should be at a relaxed and moderate pace that will train your body without going too far.

The right pace should get your heart rate up to approximately 70 percent of its maximum. But you naturally won't be able to monitor that as your run. Instead, what you implement is the Talk Test. You will know if your pace is correct when you can still talk in complete sentences while running.

The Right Form

Running is an individual sport, which means that people tend to develop their own unique techniques on how to run better. The right form is basically the kind that makes you feel most comfortable as you run. Nevertheless, there are some basic safety rules that you can apply to avoid injury:

☒ Keep your head, shoulders, torso, and pelvis upright and aligned.

☒ Look ahead, not down on the ground.

☒ Shoulders should be relaxed, with the arms carried just below the chest.

☒ Hands should be relaxed, cupped loosely and passes the body at approximately waist level.

☒ Arms should move in sync with the legs. They should move forward, instead of side to side.

☒ Feet should land lightly beneath your center of gravity.

How to Breathe while Running

The more intense your running is, the more shallow and rapid your breathing will be. Just like your muscles, your lungs also need to train in order to boost their endurance. Also, breathing correctly will bring in more oxygen for the muscles.

Chest breathing is the incorrect way to breathe because it tenses the shoulders and wastes more energy. In fact, the true key to breathing correctly is called abdominal breathing. Wherein the abdomen should fill up like a balloon as you breathe in and deflate like a balloon as you breathe out.

As much as possible, breathe through your mouth because this allows for more oxygen to enter your lungs compared to your nostrils. However, this can sometimes cause a dry throat, so remember to swallow a bit in order to let your saliva lubricate your pharynx.

You should also coordinate your breathing by counting as you breathe. Beginners should start with a 2-2 pattern, wherein you breathe in for two steps forward and breathe out for another two steps forward. Slowly increase it to 3-3 and then to 4-4 as you improve your endurance.

The Hard-Easy Principle

This is a popular, albeit controversial, running technique that basically means alternating your running days between hard and easy. To be more specific, you run fast or longer than usual in one day of running, and then on the day after that you run shorter or slower than usual. To keep it balanced, you can start the week off at your usual pace and distance. The second day should then be your "hard" day, the third will be your "easy" day, and the fourth will get you back on your regular running day.

Striders

When you apply the striders (also known as the "pick-up") technique, you are training your muscles and nervous system to adapt to a fast pace without causing fatigue because it is so short.

Striders is not a difficult workout. In fact, you can incorporate it into your run about one to two times a week. It starts off with you running easy and then increasing your speed and lengthening your stride for around 15 seconds before you slow back down to a walk.

Here are the steps on how to do Striders for beginners. If this is your first time, you can start striding for 4 seconds and gradually build it up to 6 or 8 over time.

Step 1: Look for a flat surface that will enable you to run for 30 seconds at speed (approximately 250 to 300 feet).

Step 2: Start running easy, concentrating on a fast but short stride.

Step 3: Gradually build up your speed and lengthening your stride. Make sure that your upper body stays relaxed but straight. The feeling should be more of a moderated but fast pace instead of a sprint.

Step 3: Once you are 3/4 of your way into the distance, gradually lower your speed by shortening your stride until you drop down to a walk.

Step 4: Walk back to where you started striding while breathing steadily.

Step 5: Repeat the strider again.

Don't forget to do your striders, especially if you are planning to join a marathon. After all, striders is the best way to help you run faster and more smoothly.

How to Overcome Runner's Aches and Pains

Pain is inevitable in any sport. You Otherwise, always at some point experience some type of body issue, especially if you are just starting. Injuries are not fun at all, and the worst part is that it will prevent you from running.

Most injuries are triggered when the runner exerts too much effort too soon. It also comes from not listening to the body's danger signals. While pain is normal, injuries can be avoided.

Tips on How to Avoid Injuries while Running

Strengthen your body's ability to tolerate the repetitive forces that come with running by doing the following:

☒ Stretching all of the major tendons, ligaments and muscles that you use while running.

☒ Wearing the right apparel, such as runner's shoes that have adequate cushioning and are appropriate for your foot size and type, and clothes that are not constricting blood flow.

☒ Increasing your intensity and mileage at a gradual pace in order to allow the body to adapt.

☒ Running on soft ground whenever you can, such as dirt and grass.

☒ Following a running program that is suitable for your level (in your case, the beginner's program) in order to avoid overexertion.

Stay Motivated

Running doesn't just happen; you have to make an effort to stick to it. There will be times when you are excited to lace up and head on out. But there are also times when you just don't feel it. While it's alright to take a rest every now and then, the sad part about thinking that you are too tired to run is that you eventually become demotivated.

Many people have turned running into their passion, and they, too, experience feeling too bored or tired to go outside and run. However, they have overcome this obstacle because they know how to get inspired.

7

Lifestyle And Nutrition

Nutrition

The old saying that we are what we eat is one of the best ways to describe how important it is that we manage what we put in our bodies. Now I'm not saying count calories, but I am saying start reading labels. Most of us have no idea what we are putting into our bodies.

The reality of modern life is that we are influenced by the environment more than ever before. Pollution has reached record levels, and the soil we grow our foods in are depleted of nutrients. So the food we eat is less nutritious than before.

Large companies and commercial farming have also influenced the way animals are bred on farms and what they eat. These animals end up on our dinner plates. We eat them without a second thought.

I just mentioned a couple of general observations about plants and animals, but what about processed food? Well, the general rule is that almost all of it is terrible for you. There are a few exceptions but not many. We pick these things up at supermarkets, and we eat them, and they taste great. They taste great because they were engineered by scientists to taste great. Big companies pay top dollar to make sure you get foods that are designed to make your hungry again 20 minutes later. These types of foods create chaos in our bodies.

If you look at the modern rates of cancer, diabetes, and other modern diseases(find examples), then we can easily find the connection between how humans have started to eat in the last 100 years. Asian cultures like Japan has a better record than us because of their food culture.

Hormones

One of the reasons society seems out of control sometimes is that there are very few people that have studied their own bodies. Our bodies are ancient and complex. The human body is capable of extraordinary things, however, like any other system, it gets damaged if we push it into the red sometimes. This is what we as a society do all the time, and we sometimes seem surprised when we get sick, feel depressed or feel like we are getting old.

Sure we are getting older and yes we sometimes just get sick. However, we have allowed our environment to influence us on a very deep level by consistently living out of balance. This balance in our body is the hormones that we have in our bodies. When they get out of balance, all kinds of hell brakes lose.

- **Estrogen**

Over the last 30 years, men have been getting an excess of the female hormone estrogen into their bodies. Commercial farming plastic and other factors have contributed to this.

According to Scientific Studies, there are many dangers to excess estrogen:

(1)Man boobs or enlarged breasts. This is why we so many men with saggy boobs walking around.

(2)Low Sex Drive

(3)If you are struggling to get it up, then you could have excess estrogen.

(4)The risk of Strokes because of blood clots.

(5)Heart attack. This use to be a problem with older men but is becoming more common in younger men. Less testosterone and too much estrogen could damage the heart.

(6)Problems with the prostate.

(7)Low tolerance for stress.

We need some Estrogen in the male body, but an excess will cause an imbalance in the body, and then lead to disease.

- **Testosterone**

The most important male hormone is Testosterone. The importance of this hormone cannot be overstated.

The lack of testosterone is a cause of social issues in many men's lives. If you are testosterone deficient, then it could lead to problems in our relationships, health, careers and overall happiness in life. So the importance cannot be overstated.

How do we change our eating habits, balance our hormones, and improve our health?

The first thing we have to do is to change our mindset about health and wellness. In modern life, most people tend to treat symptoms when they get sick. When they feel better, they just go back to the way they lived before. I suggest we should live healthily and prevent disease. What the modern world does at the moment is treating symptoms and not the cause. This is why people keep getting sick. The medication is just masking underlying problems connected to lifestyle.

How Do We Prevent Disease and Illness?

1- Exercise

We already looked at weight training and a good form of exercise, but there are many others. Find one and start exercising consistently.

2 - Food

Well, let's start by saying that there will be some guys that will say that eating junk food is cheaper and that it's more convenient than cooking every night.

Firstly eating healthy might be a bit more expensive but the long term investment in your health and your overall improvement in your life will be worth it. If you can spend a lot of money on alcohol, then you can take that money and invest it in your health.

What should I eat?

What you put into your body is one of the most important things that you do every day. The food you eat becomes the building blocks of your body and this will affect the way you feel and how efficient your body functions.

If you get your diet right consistently you will perform better in all other areas of life. There are many gurus with different opinions on what is healthy.I will share with you what worked for me and then you can go try it out:

-Eat Real Food And Drink Lots Of Water

Stop Eating Processed Food Including Sugar. You might struggle to cut sugar if you have been eating it for years. However, if you get over the initial cravings your health will improve and you will lose weight. Avoid processed food with the exception of whey protein.

-Drink Loads Of Black Coffee

Don't believe the bad hype coffee had over the years. Real black coffee made from fresh coffee beans is good for you. Of course, it's only good for you if you don't put in the sugar and milk. So avoid the latte and other sugary coffee drinks. Drink your coffee black. After a few weeks of black coffee and no sugar, you will never drink sugar again.

-Eat Lots of Meat

Eat a lot of good quality grass-fed meat. Most of us can't hunt deer every week and get wild meat so we have to settle for grass-fed beef or lamb. If you can't afford grass-fed go for organic or just get the best meat you can. Don't believe modern propaganda. Men need meat and lots of it. A recent study found that depression rates to be higher among vegetarians than meat-eaters,so make sure you get your steak every week. Contrary to popular belief animal fats from good sources are good for you.

The foundation of your diet should be fresh and organic meat, eggs, fish, butter and berries. I know everyone can't get or afford organic food, but don't use that as an excuse to eat bad food. If you can't find organic, then eat normal meat, eggs, and fruits, it's still a lot better than processed food. Vegetables are overrated.

My diet consists mostly of the following Foods:

-Beef, Pork,Fish
  -White Rice
  -Eggs
  -Grass Fed Unsalted Butter
  -Frozen Strawberries, Blackberries, Blueberries
  -Whey Protein

You will need extra carbohydrates. My personal choice is white rice. It is reasonably healthy and will give you the extra carbs you need to deal with doing weight training.

Avoiding Soy

Soy is one of the worst things a man can put in his body. It disrupts testosterone production and spikes the production of estrogen the female hormone.

Bulletproof

One of the biggest changes in my overall health happened when I read the book the Bullet Proof Diet by Dave Asprey. His book is revolutionary in the way he scientifically approaches what we put in our bodies and how we can best optimize our health and wellness. The Bulletproof diet is most famous for the coffee and butter that made it famous. What I can say about the Bulletproof diet is that my health has never been better.

The Bulletproof diet is easy to implement, and it will improve the quality of your life.

Upgrading your nutrition goes hand in hand with exercise and like exercise is a cornerstone of quality life. Making a big change in your eating plans can seem like a big challenge regarding implementing new habits into your life and spending extra money. However your health is a priority, and you will see the benefits in all other areas of your life like your work, relationships, and overall happiness.

· 3 -Supplements

- You have to invest in high-quality supplements

I mentioned earlier the importance of regulating our hormones for optimum health. One of the reasons why we are so out of balance as men are our hormones are all messed up. They are messed up because of environmental factors and bad nutrition. This is where supplements come into the game. Why do we take supplements if we are already eating healthy? Well, like mentioned before our environment is messed up and the soil is depleted. So we need to boost our nutrition levels.

Not all supplements are equal and some are very bad for you. Avoid all multivitamins and focus on buying high-quality supplements. It might be a bit more pricey but it's worth it.

The following supplements are the essentials:

-Vitamin D
  -Magnesium
  -Vitamin K2
  -Vitamin C
  -Iodine
  -Krill Oil
  -Vitamin A

-Zinc

-B12

If you are in doubt about supplements or can't afford high-quality supplements then rather go without them.

Whey Protein

Whey protein is one of the few "muscle building" supplements that actually work and that is good for your overall health. Try and get grass-fed Whey or a high-quality brand with no soy.

Drink Less Alcohol

One of the obvious things to improve your health is to quit alcohol or reduce it. I have almost totally cut alcohol from my life and my life has totally transformed. I still drink a glass of red wine on special occasions but that is it.

Fasting

Intermittent fasting is one of the best things you can do to improve your overall health. Intermittent fasting has many benefits but lets' look at a few. For example, when you fast your body initiates important cellular repair processes. Fasting also changes hormone levels to make stored body fat more accessible. Some studies have shown intermittent fasting may enhance the body's resistance to oxidative stress. One more thing intermittent fasting will test is your mind. There is no better test than Intermittent fasting to see how strong your self-discipline is. Your mind and body will try and get you to start eating, but you have to overcome this and focus on your physical goals.

8

The Martial Way

If you have no experience in Japanese martial arts then you have probably never heard of the term Budō. Budō is a Japanese philosophy and a way of life that uses Martial Arts as a path of self-improvement. Budō can be traced back to the 17th century Japan. Back then the Samurai had come to a strange point in their evolution as a warrior class. Through many years of training as a way of life, they have come to the point where most Samurai was almost perfect swordsman. This created the problem of getting the better of your opponent.

The Samurai had already incorporated Zen into their culture by late in the 13th century. Zen meditation gave them the skill of intense focus and overcoming the fear of death. By the 17 century, Budō started to appear in the Samurai culture.

The Samurai came to the conclusion that the warriors with the superior mental and spiritual attitude were the ones that were consistently victorious. This is how Budō developed as a way of life.

Budō is the way of the warrior. All Japanese Martial arts has its roots in Budō. We can say that Budō explores through direct experience and in depth the relationship between ethics, philosophy, and religion. Budō is a way of life. Its a way of self - development, and self-exploration.

Modern Sports martial arts is not Budō. Sports martial arts has 3 aspects that are different from Budō:

(1)The goal with a sport is to determine a winner and loser. Competitors try to get medals or trophies.

(2)Sports have rules. If there were no rules then it would end with fights to the death.

(3)There are umpires to enforce the 'rules.'

So what about Budō?

Well, none of these rules exist. Of course, Budō practitioners want to be victorious but that is not the end goal. Budō is not a game and sword fights started the moment the duel was decided.

From the moment the duel was decided the warriors were starting to take actions to defeat their opponents. There is a famous story about the legendary Samurai Miyamoto Musashi. From the moment the time and date were set all kinds of battles started happening behind the scenes and many warriors died to the buildup to the duel. Mind-games were played and Musashi went into hiding to create uncertainty with his enemies. On the day of the duel, Musashi arrived 4 hours late to confuse and unnerve his opponent. He then went on to defeat him.

At another duel, Musashi arrived 3 hours early and waited and saw an ambush being planned for him. Musashi jumped out defeated his opponent and disappeared.

At the very core of Budō is the idea that you never retreat and never give up. This means the heart of Budō is courage. This means whatever the obstacle keep moving forward and persevere.

In Japanese, "Do" means the way. "Bu" means military or war. Loosely Budō can be translated as martial way or way of the warrior. In essence its a way of living life as a warrior.

So Why am I Talking To You About Budō?

Like I mentioned earlier Budō is an approach to life. Its a mindset of the warrior. Sure I get it we are not fighting duels every day or meeting someone for a street-fight. However, we walk through life in the mindset that we are doing battle every day and should be ready for whatever the universe throws our way. Practically every day in our lives we walk through the streets we look at the world the way a warrior would. We actively observe and try to be aware and vigilant. We are always ready because we understand the reality of this planet and the uncertainty that comes with it.

Does this mean we walk around with a paranoid angry attitude? No of course not. Do we walk around looking like we are at war? No, of course not. However, we are awake, aware and vigilant. We remain on guard and ready to fight in the physical or mental sense. We know in the real world with all its battles there are no rules and that only victims think the world is an innocent place. So we practice a philosophy where we made the conscious choice not to be a victim nor wait for others to help us when chaos breaks out. We take responsibility for everything. Its a form of extreme personal responsibility. It goes above and beyond normal personal responsibility and owning what we do. It means that I take ownership of not just my actions but for who I am and my own existence.

All aspects of your life get approached with the mindset of small battles happening everywhere. Battles happening at work, at home, and within your own mind. At the heart of it, you don't back down. Every battle in life you confront, evaluate and then deal with it with courage. You never back down. In this process, you observe your own actions and weaknesses and try to improve on them consistently.

Why Adopt Budō in Your Life?

By taking in life in a more direct manner will give you a deeper understanding of life. You will also get a greater understanding into yourself and your own perceived limits and how you can overcome them. By living with a Budō code teaches you at a subconscious level to claw with your fingernails with an absolute relentless attitude towards life. You will develop a spirit of never giving up and learn to run towards adversity with courage. You will become the type of person that fights until his very last breath. Self-improvement is an always present and inseparable element of Budō philosophy. Budō is consistent personal development of the character and behavior.

In Japan, they say that Budō is the way of the Buddha. This way leads you to discover your true nature and wakes you up from the trance you have been in for most of your life. You break loose from the shackles of your own ego and start walking around like the giant you truly are.

The Budō Code Has Eight virtues

-Righteousness
  -Heroic Courage
  -Benevolence/Compassion
  -Respect
  -Honesty
  -Honor
  -Duty and Loyalty
  -Self Control

Martial Arts As a Vehicle For Personal Development

If you are not a Martial Artist I want to encourage you to consider learning a martial that is both practical and challenging. There is no point in studying a martial art that is not practical in the modern world. I have a lot of respect for traditional martial arts but I do think in the modern world some martial arts are more suitable for the society we live in today where sword fighting is limited. However, I do think to prepare yourself for defense against weapons is a good idea. This book is not focused on martial arts so I will give you my recommendations and a few options to consider. Its then up to you to do some research and make a choice on what martial art is a good fit for you.

There is no better tool than a martial art for all-round human development. It will challenge you and expose your physical and mental weaknesses. It will then put you in the position to either face those weaknesses or retreat. If you decide to live the Budō approach to life then you will confront those weaknesses both on and off the mat. You will attack life directly. You will stop hiding from life and start living with spirit and courage.

Gracie Jiu-Jitsu

My martial art of choice is Gracie Jiujitsu or the more common name Brazilian Jiu-Jitsu (BJJ). The term Brazilian Jiu-Jitsu is a broad term for the more sports orientated form of Jiu-Jitsu. However, Gracie Jiu-Jitsu is a more traditional form of the same art and has its primary focus on the self-defense aspect of the martial art. Gracie Jiu-Jitsu will teach you how to defend yourself and put you on a path of personal development. The Gracie Academy would be my recommendation if you choose to start training Jiu-Jitsu. Unfortunately most modern Jiu-Jitsu academies these days just focus on sport and therefore loses the heart of what Jiu-Jitsu is all about.

The next part of this chapter will be a more detailed look into Jiu-Jitsu so you have a better understanding of Jiu-Jitsu. However, if you choose a different route then that is fine. There are many martial arts out there that are great to develop you as a human. Martial arts like Judo, Karate, Muay Thai are also great Self Defense systems.

Jiu Jitsu (BJJ)

The world at large didn't know anything about Brazilian Jiu-Jitsu before Royce Gracie and the first four Ultimate Fighting Championship tournaments. Nevertheless, the core concept of the UFC tournament was shared by the founders of this martial art. Brazilian Jiu-Jitsu (or BJJ) was catapulted to fame when the skinny Gracie won the first, second, as well as the fourth UFC tournaments fighting like a human anaconda that even relatively larger men feared.

Type of Art

BJJ is at its core a grappling martial art. It is a full-contact sport and competitions do not usually employ the usual safety gear such as helmets, shin guards, soft body armour, or even gloves. Although BJJ practitioners taking part in mixed martial arts do wear gloves, those who compete in pure BJJ competitions do not wear them.

The emphasis of this martial art is basically fighting on the ground. Studies show that the majority of all one on one hand to hand combats usually end up on the ground. Some estimate it from 60 to 80 percent of any street fight or aggressive encounter.

This is basically where Brazilian Jiu-Jitsu shines where other traditional martial arts rarely put any emphasis. On the ground strength, size, and reach are rendered ineffective. Both the larger and smaller combatants are on equal footing when the fight is moved to the ground.

History

Brazilian Jiu-Jitsu is popularly attributed to the Gracie family. However, it was Mitsuyo Maeda who brought the original martial art from Japan to the shores of Brazil. Maeda traveled the world to spread Japanese JiuJitsu and more so Judo. He slowly perfected his craft as he pitted his skills against practitioners of other martial arts.

Some of the skilled opponents that Maeda fought against included practi-tioners of savate, wrestlers, and even boxers. He arrived in Brazil on 14th of November 1914. While in Brazil, Maeda demonstrated his art to the local folks via the Queirolo Brothers' circus. This was where Carlos Gracie would first catch a glimpse of this martial art and fall in love with it forever.

Carlos studied Judo under the direct tutelage of Maeda. He learned this martial art for several years. He also passed his knowledge along to his brothers. Carlos' brother Helio slowly developed Brazilian Jiu Jitsu from the craft taught to him by his brother.

He had to adapt the martial art to his situation – he could not execute some of the moves employed in Judo, especially the ones that required one to oppose the strength of an opponent. His adaptations focused more on ground fighting. It basically turned the art into a form that is practical even for a smaller or weaker fighter.

Note that the Gracies are not the only originators of Brazilian Jiu Jitsu. Maeda had other students. One of them was Luiz Franca and is represented today by his students beginning with Oswaldo Fadda. The popular Brazil-based mixed martial arts team Nova Uniao, where dominant champions like Jose Aldo hail from, lean toward Fadda's BJJ style, which dominantly focuses on foot locks.

<u>Strong Points</u>

The strong points of this martial art are in its ground fighting. The fight is neutralized for both combatants, and the encounter is transformed as it were into a mechanical chess game on the floor. The more knowledgeable fighter fighting on his back eventually wins despite the lack of size or strength.

There are a lot of manoeuvres that can be used by the disadvantaged combatant. Since a fight will most likely end up on the ground, a smaller or weaker opponent should expect to end up on his back eventually. If you don't know how to defend yourself while lying on your back, then expect the fight to end in a few moments.

However, this is where Brazilian JiuJitsu turns things around. Even if you are the weaker opponent, you can still take advantage of your position and attack even when your opponent is right on top of you. There are many ways you can strangle, lock, neutralize, and even break your opponent even if you are on your back. The philosophy is that when the fight moves into the ground phase, then both opponents are on equal footing. This is where knowledge of ground fighting comes into prominence in real life combat.

Practicality

There are a lot of practical applications of Brazilian JiuJitsu. It is very easy for anyone to admit that there is always someone who is stronger and bigger than you are. So, basing your martial arts skill on pure strength and size is in itself a self-defeating endeavor.In a street situation, BJJ is very practical and efficient.For people with limited physical strength, this martial art is a great fit.

Weaknesses

One of the fundamental flaws of Brazilian Jiu Jitsu is its entire lack of striking skills. Even though BJJ is demonstrably effective against traditional stand-up fighting techniques, there are ways to counter the attempts of a BJJ practitioner to take his opponent down to the ground.

Experience shows that a purely BJJ-based fighter or a purely stand up based fighter or striker can be outmatched by a well-rounded mixed martial artist. BJJ in the end requires something to balance its pure ground game, and that can come from other effective stand up fighting arts mentioned in this book.

Aikido

You may have first seen the art of Aikido demonstrated in one of Steven Seagal's movies. It may have been quite an impressive thing to see him defeat five or more opponents with just a few simple strokes of his hands. He even defeats them in stunning fashion – some get thrown, others get broken limbs, and a few getting mortally wounded.

You may even recognize some of the throws and moves as a form of Judo or Jujutsu. Aikido was derived from these martial arts, which are its ancestors. After admitting that fact, an Aikidoka (Aikido practitioner) will also quickly add that his art is a lot smoother compared to the former arts.

Type of Art

Most will classify Aikido as a form of grappling art. Its main emphasis is in throws, pretty much like Judo, but it also has an equal emphasis on joint locks. Another signature of this martial art is the use of the opponent's momentum and not your strength. This is achieved using techniques in turning as well as entering thus diverting the direction of the opponent's force and neutralizing an attack.

History

The art of Aikido was created by Morihei Ueshiba. Just like other traditional martial arts from nation of Japan, this one also reflects the philosophy and religious views of its maker. The name Aikido simply means "The Way of Unifying the Life Energy."

The meaning behind the name of this combat system describes the overall approach it takes to win combat. And that is to blend your opponent's strength with that of yours and use both to win in combat. With that philosophy in mind, the Aikidoka will only need to use a small amount of his own strength to defeat his opponent.

Ueshiba developed his combat art and system in the period of 1920 to 1930. He synthesized the martial arts that he learned at the time into one system. At the very core of this martial art is Daitō-ryū aiki-jūjutsu, which Ueshiba studied directly under the hands of the famed Takeda Sōkaku.

In 1901 Ueshiba is also known to have studied under the renowned master of Tenjin Shin'yō-ryū by the name of Tozawa Tokusaburō. From 1903 to 1908, he was under the tutelage of Nakai Masakatsu as he studied Gotōha Yagyū Shingan-ryū. And in 1911 he learned Judo under Kiyoichi Takagi.

These martial arts have similarities as well as differences in principle, style, and approach. Nevertheless, Ueshiba leans towards Daitō-ryū as he developed the system which he will later call Aikido. Note that Ueshiba didn't merely focus on empty handed or barehanded combat methods. In fact, a huge section of his instructions dealt in the use of weapons particularly the sword.

The actual date when Ueshiba introduced Aikido is unknown, unfortunately. However, it is also known that he used to call this fighting system as Aiki Budo. The earliest usage of the name "Aikido" as an official name of this fighting system is in the year 1942.

Aikido spread throughout the world beginning in 1951 in France. In 1953 a martial arts tour was conducted in the United States. In that tour, Kenji Tomiki had the opportunity to demonstrate aikido in 15 US states. It was presented along with other prominent martial arts at the time.

However, it was Koichi Tohei who set up the first dojos in the United States in the islands of Hawaii. This was the first formal introduction of this combat art in the US.

Other practitioners and masters of the art were sent as official representatives and delegates of this art to different countries of the world. Nevertheless, the largest Aikido organisation in the world is still the Aikikai Foundation, which is primarily run by the Ueshiba family. It should be noted that just like other martial arts, there are also variants and styles within Aikido. You may encounter one school that teaches one particular style which is different from what is taught in another – nevertheless, they all follow the same fundamental techniques and principles.

Strong Points

The strength of Aikido is in its focus in using your enemy's strength against him. The techniques used in Aikido resemble judo in certain aspects. An Aikidoka doesn't need to be the strongest warrior. He or she only needs to be the one who can better channel an opponent's force.

Techniques and moves in Aikido especially in self-defense can be used and mastered even by those who are obviously weaker and smaller. There aren't that many known tournaments in Aikido (except of course the few conducted by Shodokan Aikido) due to the fact that the moves, locks, throws, and breaks of aikido can be lethal.

Practicality

Aikido is a great option for smaller or weaker practitioners. You will basically rely in your knowledge of using your opponent's momentum against him. It is also a good option for those who are faced with multiple opponents.

Weaknesses

Aikido has been criticized with regard to the counter-maneuvers it presents. Some say that the attacks made by strikers including punches, kicks, and armed strikes are easy to deflect. Critics go on to say that if the supposed attacks practiced in the dojo are flimsy then the student will not understand how to defend himself in real life combat.

This critique is heavily debated. Those from the Shodokan Aikido school have demonstrated that aikido can be used in actual combat and in competitive format as well. However, there are sectors within the Aikido organization who are against competitive formats saying that it departs from the spirit of this combat art since it is not only a martial art or game, but a spiritual philosophy as well.

Muay Thai

Muay Thai is a martial art that hails from Thailand. Some people compare this combat art form to kickboxing, but there definitely are differences in both disciplines. Muay Thai at its core is both a physical as well as a mental discipline. It has become one of the more popular martial arts today.

Type of Art

This is one of the martial arts in this book that primarily focuses on a stand-up game. It's a striking art and some people may call it boxing mixed with a kicks and knees. However, another huge aspect of this martial art is clinch-fighting. Practitioners make use of the clinch to inflict powerful critical strikes against an opponent. That includes attacks using one's elbows using efficient angles to inflict more damage. In effect, it is not merely a distance striking art – it is also a form of close quarter combat.

History

Muay Thai has a long history that spans hundreds of years into the Thailand's past. It was initially a bare fisted fighting system used in ancient warfare. It eventually evolved as a type of competition among practitioners during local festivals that are usually held in temples. This fighting art became the main component of the fighting style used in the year 1560 under the reign of then King Naresuan.

The golden age of Muay Thai came along in 1868 under the reign of Rama V. This time, the king himself was interested in this combat art. Muay Thai started to be seen as a form of exercise as well as a type of martial art.

Starting in 1935 competition rules were established. The very first boxing rings for Muay Thai were established during this time. Referees were then included as a third man on the ring, just like in the case of boxing. The entire match was also divided into several periods also known as rounds.

The traditional hemp rope that was wrapped around the hands of fighters was replaced by boxing gloves. Later on, groin protectors, as well as coverlets made of cotton on the fighter's feet, were also added into the protective gear used in matches.

Muay Thai today has become a very popular sport all over the world. In fact, it is a staple in many mixed martial arts tournaments. It has been demonstrated to be effective against many classical striking arts including Taekwondo and

Karate.

Strong points

A fighter will not only rely on his hands or feet when using Muay Thai. Kicks with knees and punches with elbows are effective tools to inflict the most amount of damage on an opponent. This is also why they call this fighting style as the Art of Eight Limbs. Your hands or feet can get hurt or damaged when used to strike against an opponent, but that won't stop a nak muay (i.e. a Muay Thai practitioner). The elbows, as well as the knees, are just as effective. Other than that, you can also use clinch fighting and defeat your opponent in close range.

A Muay Thai practitioner can employ pretty unconventional strikes compared to boxing and other pure fist striking sports and martial arts. Everyone is familiar with a jab, cross, and a hook. You may have even seen these punches thrown in odd angles.

However, a spinning back fist, cobra punch, or even a wild swing may come from an angle not familiar to most people. Elbow strikes such as horizontal, slash, reverse, uppercut, mid-air elbow strikes, spinning elbows, and horizontal elbow strikes will come as a surprise to any opponent, especially in a clinch situation.

Knees are also effective especially when in the clinch. Knee strikes include horizontal knee strikes, diagonal, straight, flying knee, curving knee strike, knee bomb, and step up knee strikes. They are also effective in close range and clinch fights.

Another strong point of Muay Thai is clinch-fighting. Some of the clinches used in this martial art include the swan neck, arm clinch, low clinch, and the side clinch. Once a clinch has been applied to an opponent, elbows and knees can be effectively used to inflict a lot of damage.

Practicality

Many of the strikes employed in Muay Thai can be executed by anyone with enough practice. This art can serve as an effective form of self-defense if you don't have any available weapons. Practitioners can also use this martial art to defend against multiple opponents.

Weaknesses

The drawbacks of Muay Thai are pretty much similar to any stand-up fighting system. Once the phase of the combat goes to the ground, then the Muay Thai practitioner will have no solid training or background in counterattacking a well-versed ground fighter. It should be repeated here that a huge percentage of all combat encounters eventually end up on as a match on the ground.

A Muay Thai practitioner, on the other hand, can cope with grapplers by applying take down defenses, which includes sprawling and maintaining a balanced stand-up position. This means that a practitioner of this art should incorporate a bit of ground defense in order to negate any attempts of an opponent to bring the fight on the ground.

Another downside of Muay Thai is that it has very little support for smaller and weaker fighters. This fighting system favors those who can strike harder and faster. Another issue is that a fighter that has a longer reach can have a significant advantage. A younger and stronger Muay Thai fighter has a significant advantage over a weaker opponent.

Judo

The name Judo literally means the "way of gentleness" or "the gentle way." But if you consider the techniques employed by this martial art, the general public would think that there is nothing gentle about it. It is a popular martial art and sport that eventually became part of the Olympics since the year 1964.

The art of Judo has taken the spotlight once again in the world of mixed martial arts. Some of the competitors in this newly developed sport have a Judo background. One of the most successful Judoka (Judo practitioner) of late is Ronda Rousey

Rousey won the Ultimate Fighting Championship's Women's Bantamweight belt; successfully defeating almost every opponent on the ground and with a signature finish – an armbar. Other popular figures in the world of Judo include Hector Lombard, Kayla Harrison, Fedor Emelianenko, Jimmy Pedro (instructor at the Olympic Training Center in Massachusetts), Hidehiko Yoshida, Yoshihiro Akiyama, and Vladimir Putin.

<u>Type of Art</u>

Even though Judo is basically a grappling art, its emphasis is in throws. In competitions, a match can be ended by executing a throw, or it can be finished via a grappling match on the ground. But throws and takedowns are the art's most prominent features.

On the ground, pinning techniques can be applied by a Judo practitioner to either subdue or at least immobilize an opponent. Joint locks, as well as chokes, are utilized in this martial art as well.

Some may not immediately agree that this combat art is entirely a ground fighting system since a lot of the techniques primarily focus on the stand-up phase and the takedown phase of an actual combat. However, striking and weapons defense are an integral part of the art. Students are actually taught how to use the principles of Judo as a self-defense in real life situations including threats from an armed opponent.

<u>History</u>

Judo was created by Jigoro Kano, who was also an educator. He studied jujutsu under different masters or teachers which included Fukuda Hachinosuke, Iso Masatomo, Iikubo Tsunetoshi. Each sensei (teacher) focused on different aspects of the art of jujutsu that included randori (freestyle practice), kata (pre-arranged combat forms), and nage-waza (throwing techniques).

Kano founded his own school in 1882. His teachings are both philosophical as well as combat oriented. He emphasized the achievement of maximum efficiency with the use of minimal effort. He also emphasized mutual benefit in combat where both parties in the fight learn from one another. One of his foremost teachings is that gentleness controls hardness.

Competitions were an integral part of Jujutsu and Judo. Even Jigoro Kano became a competition chairperson as early as 1899. Committees were made to create contest rules to regulate matches. Rules continued to be added in later years.

In 1930, the first All Japan Judo Championship was held. The World Judo Championships were first held in 1956. The first ever Women's Championships were organized in the year 1980. Judo was first incorporated into the Olympics in 1964 and the first women's Judo event in the Olympics was held in 1988.

Strong Points

The strength of Judo is in its takedowns and ground game. Locks and chokeholds follow after putting the enemy effectively on the ground. If you want to solidify your takedown skills, then the best way to do it is to learn from one of the best Judokas in the business.

It is not primarily a striking art (i.e. punching and kicking) although it does incorporate some of the strikes in the kata. If faced with an opponent that has no background against a grappler, a Judoka can immediately gain the upper hand. A Judoka doesn't have to be the stronger, larger, or faster opponent to prevail in a match.

This aspect of this martial art was demonstrated even when Judo was pitted against its predecessor art of Jujutsu. This is one of the reasons why Judo was adopted as the national martial art of Japan in the 1800s. A demonstration of

Judo against other combat art forms also convinced law enforcement officers in the country to make it as the martial art used by police officers and even in the military.

Practicality

One of the strengths of Judo is in its thrust or emphasis in the application of its techniques in realistic combat situations. Jigoro Kano highly favors the use of randori, or free form practice, although he too practices kata. This type of practice exposes a Judoka to situations that are not usually experienced during competition or a match in a dojo. In that aspect, Judo has the potential to evolve and transform into a broader art.

The techniques used in Judo can be used by older folks and even young children. Some of the techniques may require one to oppose the strength or momentum of an opponent, but many of aspects of the art practically makes use of your opponent's force, weight, and strength against him.

Weaknesses

One of the bigger drawbacks of Judo is pretty much the same with any grappling form of art. It's reduced emphasis on striking presents a particular weakness in the art. It tries to compensate for this lack by teaching students how to defend against strikers. However, it should be noted that a striker who has a pretty good takedown defense can prevent any attacks by a Judoka and make use his superior striking skills to take advantage of a combat situation.

9

Managing Ourselves

The key to Self Discipline that leads to a very high level of success is managing your time and personal productivity. In order for you to use self-discipline that leads to success, you need 2 elements to get you there. The first part is you feeling happy and content internally. And the second part is you effectively and relentlessly executing on your goals.

These 2 elements are like yin and yang to each other. They keep each other in balance and can't exist without each other. Think about this reality for a second. If you feel happy and positive inside but you don't have a mission and purpose in life then you will feel incomplete and slowly but surely your happiness will disappear.

On the other hand, if you have goals and a mission in life but you feel empty and negative on the inside then your goals and mission will start falling apart and become meaningless. Everything in the universe works in this type of yin and yang balance. You can't have hot without cold and hard without soft. This is the nature of the universe. This is also the nature of success.

So how do we make sure we stay happy but also stay very productive?

You Need To Create Your Startup Ritual

What is a startup ritual? A startup ritual is my list of actions I take every morning to start my day. Rituals or habits are very powerful.I already illustrated the power of habits in a previous chapter. I shared with you the story of Micheal Phelps the Olympic champion and how he used success habits and rituals to train his brain to become successful.

This startup ritual works very well because it sets the tone for the rest of the day. Once you execute your startup ritual the rest of the day gets so much easier. Your startup ritual makes you hit the ground running and makes the rest of the day so much easier.

So what should you include in your morning startup ritual? To create your ritual think about all the things that would empower you mentally, emotionally and physically?

Let's start by setting your alarm clock for 5:30 am. You want to be done with your ritual at 7 am. So you have an hour and a half for your startup ritual.

You can put whatever worked for you in your ritual. But I will share with you my ritual to give you an idea of how this works:

-Alarm Rings at 5:30. I get up to wash my face and brush my teeth.

-Drink a glass of cold water

-Make a cup Of Coffee

-Sit down, read my vision and goals

-Write down my goals on a piece of paper

-Finish my coffee and go sit down in a comfortable position

-Visualize my vision

-Zazen Meditation

-Yoga

-After Yoga, I make a berry protein shake for breakfast.

-Take a shower

-Start the day

Be very specific about your ritual. For example what type of shake will it be? Will it be organic with green powder? Be very specific and tailor-make your ritual to empower you. If you design your ritual into a powerhouse then you will be unstoppable the rest of the day. Unfortunately, most people start their day in chaos and the rest of the day they are just reacting and putting out fires. But if you have a startup ritual you will feel in total control of your day. The whole idea is to start your day with a lot of positive momentum.

Alignment

To create maximum productivity in your life you need to align everything in your life so it's all focused on your mission. To illustrate this point let's look at the following example. Let's say a guy wants to be an Olympic Swimmer. So the guy starts swimming every week and going to the gym. But he also has a drinking habit twice a week. Those 2 nights he parties and drinks a lot of alcohol. He enjoys his time with friends.But he fails in his goal because he is not aligned with his mission.

To reach your goals and achieve your vision for your life you need to align all the parts of your life. You can't say you want to achieve something great but parts of you are not aligned with that goal.

Go sit down and make 2 lists. The first list is your most important goals. Your second list is the things you spent the most time on. If the second list is not matching your goals then you are out of alignment. You need to be hard on yourself if you want to reach your goals. There are no compromises in this game.

Work In Single Focus Blocks Of 60 Minutes

Human focus has two parts. The first part is the quantity and the second part is quality. When you combine these 2 parts you get powerful results. So let's start with the quality and quantity part of the focus.

The quantity is the time you spent doing something. The quality is the thing that you choose to do within that time. This might seem obvious to many but there is big power with the right combination of both quantity and quality.

Let's start with time. You need to set a single block of time for your work of 60 minutes. The key is that this is an uninterrupted time.No smartphone, phone calls or any other distraction. We live in a time with a lot of distractions and most people have minds that are out of control. They cannot focus one thing for longer than 5 minutes. This is a problem and if you struggle to focus then start with a thirty-minute block of work and then build that focus up to an hour. After an hour take a 20 min break relaxing.

Don't surf the net or check your phone. Go for a walk or take a short nap. Then make a cup of coffee and start with your next 60 min block of time. Try and build up those 60 min blocks. If you struggle with focus then try and do 3 blocks and build it up to 6 blocks. Do whatever it takes to build up those blocks of focus.

The second part of building this focus muscle is to decide what it is you will focus on. In other words the quality part of your focus. A lot of people do a lot of "work" but don't accomplish much because they spend their time on the wrong things. You need to go sit down and make a list of the most important things in your life. Think about the things that will give you the most leverage over the next 5 years and longer. For example, physical training every day will give you long term health benefits. Working on creating content for your business will grow your company and make you money. Then break it down further. For example, weight training will give the most benefits so that is one block of time. Building my website will make me a lot of money so that is another block of time.

So you have to objectively look at your life and ask yourself what is the most important work you will focus on? This will be the quality part of your focus.

Time

Time is your most important commodity. Once it's gone you will never get it back. So use it wisely and start looking at how you spend your time. You have to manage your time efficiently. Plan everything. This means your days, weeks and hours. You have to become very deliberate in the way you live.

You need to observe your days, weeks and months to figure out where you are wasting time. Start writing down how many hours you sleep and manage it accordingly. You don't need more than 6 hours of sleep a night.

Organization

You need to manage your house, car, office, computer, email, social media so that you are in control. Don't allow these variables to control you. You have the power to control these things. It's up to you to create order in them. You have to be organized in all these areas or they will affect everything else you do. Keep everything clean, crisp and in its place.

Goals and Vision

In life, you need a vision. This means you need to know where you are going otherwise you are on the road to nowhere. If you don't have a vision for your life it's like driving a car without a map. You are just driving without really going anywhere.

After you have set up your vision you need to set up your goals. Break those big goals down into monthly goals so that you can track your progress. Go over your goals every morning before work and every night before you go to sleep. The best way to do this is to write it down every day on a blank piece of paper. This way these goals get driven deep into your subconscious mind so you constantly feel the need to take action on them.

Executing Consistently

You need to become a relentless executing machine. Take massive action towards your goals and vision. Stay focused and stay the course. Don't take your eye off your goals. Follow your plan and don't let anyone get you off your path and your mission. The resistance will come to try and stop you. People will try and stop you. Your emotions will try and stop you, failures will try and stop you, your mind will try and stop you. But above it all, you must rise up like a king and dominate. Dominate like a warrior armed with the great big sword of Self Discipline.

Preparation

Make sure you are ready for every day by being prepared. Make sure your alarm clock is set for the next day. Get your bags packed and clothes ready to put on. Prepare your breakfast and set it up for an easy exit. You need to hit the ground running. Remember, "Victory loves preparation."

Taking Time out

On Sundays take a day off to rest and reflect. Most importantly take 20 min and practice some gratitude. This might sound a bit corny but it's necessary to stay grounded and focused. Be grateful for what you have achieved so far but also recognize that you can do a lot more. Spend the day relaxing and spending time with your loved ones like your girlfriend/wife/family/kids.

10

Finding Focus

The world will resist your efforts. You need to build a mindset based on an incredibly strong focus. Your vision should be in your mind constantly and at the same time, you need to let it go by focusing on long-term goals and monthly goals. This will drive you. This focus will be your superpower.

You need to funnel everything you do every day into this funnel of discipline. Meditation ,exercise,diet,sacrifice etc.It all funnels into your self Disciplined focus. It all comes together in this machine of focus. Your focus is building on your Self Discipline.

All your daily actions and choices are building your culture of control and self-discipline. Your mindset is where you bring it all together. You know that Self Discipline is the tool to live a life of success and abundance.

The way you think about daily life is going to be massively important.

The Power Of Positive thinking

Don't worry I'm not telling you to blindly think the world is always a nice place because we all know that is not true. What I am telling you is that positivity has incredible power to drive you forward and push closer to your vision. Staying Disciplined every day, every week and every year can become draining if you don't frame it all in a positive light. Yea I get it, a lot of bad stuff happens, but we all have a choice every day. A choice to see the positive or the negative. We choose what we focus on.

A lot of people quit Self-discipline and with that goes all their dreams and goals. One of the big reasons for this is that they focus on the negative side of their experiences. They could have focused on the positive but the negative was so tempting that they gave into it. The truth about negativity is that there is such an abundance of it that you never have a hard time to find a lot of it. It's everywhere you go. Negativity on the news, social media, gossip, etc.It 95% negative.

For example, you go to the gym and you get tortured by your personal trainer. You hurt and for the next few days, you are in pain.A little voice starts telling you "That trainer is too harsh. I don't need this in my life." Or your friends start saying things like "We like the old you better" or "Why do you want to do Weight training?"So all these negative thoughts, statements, and emotions are suddenly in abundance. Most people give in to them. But what if you changed the frame to the positive? What if you listened to the positive voice?The one that says "If I keep this up I will lose all this fat and look great" or "If I get through this pain I will get the body I want and get my confidence back."What if you focused on this positive voice? Well, the answer is simple. You won't quit. You will keep on going. You will accept the pain and keep your discipline.

What you focus on is a choice. You will have to make these little choices daily and consistently. The easiest way to get through them is to focus on the positive frame.

Build a Ritual Of Focus

By now you should have written out your vision for your life and all your goals. Every morning you wake up and take a shower. Then make a cup of coffee. Go sit down and take out your journal with your vision and goals. While sipping on your coffee start reading your vision out loud to yourself. Do this 3 times.

After you finished reading your vision take a look at your goals. Do the same thing. Read your goals out loud for yourself. Then take a pen and write out your goals 3 times on a piece of paper. The exercise of writing your goals down every morning will cement them in your mind.

Now finish your coffee and go sit or lie down in a comfortable place. Put on some nice relaxing music. It has to be relaxing music with no words to put you in a trance. Now close your eyes. Start visualizing your vision of your life and see yourself already achieving all those things in your life vision. Take 10 minutes for this part of the exercise. Then visualize for another 10 minutes how you successfully achieve all your goals. For example, if you want to climb Mount Everest. See yourself at the top of the summit smiling and then safely going down. Feel the cold air on your face and the sun in your eyes. Use all your senses and let the music take you away and stir your creativity. Don't think this is some pointless exercise. Visualization is one of the most powerful exercises you can do.

Like I mentioned in a previous chapter Elite Special Forces and elite Athletes use visualization to train their minds to stay disciplined and reach their objectives. The mind can not differentiate between the pictures in your mind and reality. By doing this you are training your subconscious mind to get in the habit of being successful.

Only Think About The Next 5 Minutes

A lot of people are not successful because they get overwhelmed by the big picture. They think about the massive task in front of them and they freeze. Elite athletes like Micheal Jordan says that he used to only focus on the next play, he never thought about what was at stake. He said that if players started thinking about winning championships their focus wasn't in the game. So whenever you are starting something new or taking a new direction in life don't get overwhelmed and turn it into this big thing in your mind. All you have to do is think about the next 5 minutes and then the next 5 minutes after that.

Special Operations candidates have to go through the brutal selection and training courses to eventually qualify as a Special Operations Operator. For example, a Green Beret Special Forces candidate has to go through the Special Forces Selection course, the Qualification Course, language school, survival school, airborne school and some go through Ranger School. This takes up to 2 years or even more. Almost 70% of candidates don't make it through the 2 year period.

At the beginning of this period, candidates can get overwhelmed at the mountain that lies ahead and the reality of the odds against them. During this time the fear of the mental and physical mountain ahead makes many candidates start doubting themselves. The candidates are taught to only focus on the next 5 minutes. The 5-minute rule will get you through situations that you thought were not possible by placing your focus on the now and the next 5 minutes.

Let Go Of Things You Can't Control

There are some things in life you can't control. It's natural for the human mind to start wondering and start thinking about things outside its reach. If something is out of your control then let it go. Don't make yourself sick with worry. If you start thinking about these things then stop. Bring your mind back to what you are doing right now and start thinking about the next 5 minutes.

Open Sets

In life, we start things and we don't finish them. Or we get ourselves into situations that we don't deal with. For example, you start writing a book but never finish it. Or you get into an argument with someone and never resolve the conflict. These are open sets in your mind. These open sets plague your mind and mess with your focus. You need to deal with these issues and resolve them. When you do this you will remove weight off your shoulders. For example, finish the book you were writing or go and talk to the person you are arguing with and resolve it. Done.

Focus On What You Want To Achieve In Life Not What You Want To Avoid

A lot people make the mistake of taking actions to avoid a certain outcome. What they should be doing is just focusing on the positive outcome. The subconscious mind will start going towards a negative outcome if you focus on it. Think big and think about your ideal outcome. Your target is all that matters.

11

The Secret Of Sacrifice

A large part of Self Discipline is built on sacrifice. Sacrifice is a very important component of self-discipline. But it's also the key to getting everything you want in life. Giving things up now so you can live your dream life.

Remember this. You can have anything you want in life but you can't have everything. You need to make some important choices and you will have to let some things go. You will have to let many things go so you can reach your goals in life and reach your full potential.

Some people never get what they want in life because they get seduced by choice. Choice is one of our greatest gifts. However, within this gift is a hidden danger. This danger is not making a choice on what you will focus on. I see this all the time, guys want to make a change but they can't choose one thing so they chase many targets at once. The problem is they never catch any of them and achieve nothing. For example, you can't say you want to start a business but also start studying for a Masters's degree in Science. You have to choose one and go after it with everything you got.

I asked you earlier in this book what is your "why"? Why do you want to be Self Disciplined? We all have reasons for bringing discipline into our lives. There is immense value in Self-Discipline just by itself. Just as a tool for survival on this planet. However, I know if you are reading this book you have giant goals you want to achieve and an even bigger vision for your future. Self Discipline will be the vehicle to get you those things. For you to get those things you need to make friends with sacrifice. More than friends, you need to embrace it.

How badly do you want to reach your goals? Is it just something you dabble in? Or is it an absolute must for you? It's easy to talk and be the man at the parties. We all know that guy. The guy who is always talking about those great things he is going to do but he never takes any actions to achieve it. If you ask him about it a year later he will have some excuse to why he didn't do it. The reason why most of these men fail is that they are not willing to give it all up. They are not willing to sacrifice to get what they want. They are not willing to embrace their friend self-discipline. These men choose instant gratification over long term victories. These men are afraid of pain and run at the first sight of shadows. The big talkers show their true colors when you confront them and ask them about their results.

Sacrifice is the fuel you put into your car that takes you toward your vision. Every-time you sacrifice something for the greater good of your mission you put in more fuel and your engine runs stronger and more powerful.You start driving longer distances and drive all over the place in your car. This car is has a name. It's called success.

Next Level Discipline

The fact that you are reading this book means you mean business.You are serious about success and you want to reach your goals. You are not willing to sacrifice on that. Your obsession with your mission drives you to do whatever it takes to get what you want. You know that in order for you to win you need to study the masters.

You need to study the GOATS as they say in the NBA. The GOATS are the greatest of all time. If you think of GOATS in basketball you think of guys like Kobe and MJ. If you think about GOATS in business think of Elon Musk, Peter Thiel, and Grant Cardone to name a few. There are GOATS in all fields. Whatever fields you are in you need to find the GOATS and study them? Read their biographies and find out as much as possible from them. Then ask yourself what can you learn from them and implement it in your own life.

Motivation is not enough

Like I mentioned earlier in this chapter motivation is not enough to get you there. You need to go sit down and figure out your reason for doing this. Then sit down and write it down on a piece of paper. Read it every morning when you get up and every night before you go to bed.

So What Do we need if Motivation Is Not Enough?

I love motivation, it gives me that much-needed boost every now and then. However, there is something else more powerful than just motivation. This thing has gotten a very bad reputation but it's one of the most powerful things in the universe if you use it right.

This thing is an obsession. Are you obsessed with your mission? Are you obsessed with your purpose?

I don't understand the big generalization people make about being obsessed.I mean people are sometimes obsessed with things that do nothing for them or things that are very bad for them. Then people don't really give criticism for those things. For example, when someone is obsessed with some TV show which they obsessively watch then people joke about it and think it's cool. If someone smokes a lot of cigarettes nobody stops that person and says "Hey I think you are a bit obsessed with that smoking thing".But as soon as someone works a lot and absolutely loses himself in his mission on this planet people have a problem with it. Suddenly people are concerned and say things like "You need more balance in your life".Or "you need to take a break".Another good one is "You are an obsessive work-person".Well, yes I am an obsessive work-person. I am obsessed with my success and potential. Why is that a bad thing?

Motivation is not something that keeps you up at night, but obsession does. It's something that is always in your mind. When you go to the gym, take a shower, or go for a run. It's always there. Your purpose consumes you.

What are You Willing To Give Up To Get What You Want?

How obsessed are you with your mission and what are you willing to give up to get it. When you become so obsessed with your mission that it consumes you people will judge you. They will try to stop you. They don't understand that your drive comes from a deep and meaningful place. Your vision is so large that nothing less than total obsession will get you there. They don't understand that your "selfish" behavior is to accomplish your vision. And when your vision becomes a reality you will change the world. They won't understand it and don't expect them to understand it. You will realize that Self-Discipline and sacrifice can become a very lonely road. But you accept that. You know this in itself is the sacrifice. You have to be willing to do whatever it takes to reach your goals.

When I started implementing extreme self-discipline into my life I annoyed a lot of people. I didn't do anything to other people, however, my obsession with my mission made them freak out. They resented my extreme focus and dedication. They started hating me for saying no to all the party invites and social gatherings. They started hating me for going to the gym when they were drinking. They got annoyed when I didn't show up for new year celebrations. They got annoyed with it all.

They didn't understand that I was willing to give it all up. I gave up my social life, alcohol, parties, junk food, hobbies and I even later moved to a different country to go after my goals. I was resented for everything. But that was what I was willing to sacrifice to get what I wanted.

My focus every day is on keeping my self-discipline. This discipline gives me the freedom to be obsessed with my vision and goals. I am 180% invested in myself. The irony about Self Discipline is that extreme levels of Self Discipline and sacrifice give you everything you ever wanted.

The bottom line is this: Self-Discipline will set you free.

Like I mentioned earlier in the book, you need to observe your days, weeks, and months to figure out where you are wasting time. If something is not aligned with your mission. Then cut the cord and sacrifice it all.

Comfort Zones Will Be Your Enemy

When you first start making self-discipline part of your life you will see some improvements. However, the danger will be if you fall into the trap of the comfort zone. For example, earlier in my life, I made some improvements in my life and I got a job that was comfortable and the pay was decent. I made good money and I got comfortable. I got so much comfort that I got stuck. I was just getting my money and living out my days without making any real improvements. I thought I was good.

Before I knew it 4 years had passed and I was still in that job and had saved no money. I was spending, going on vacation and had been seduced by comfort. My self-discipline went out the door and I got lost in the comfort zone. The thing about a comfort zone is that you don't see it coming. It sneaks up on you and before you know it you have drowned in the comfort. The lesson in this story is to never get too comfortable. When you get to a point where you feel like you are "good" then take that as a signal that you are vulnerable. Don't get seduced by a little success or progress. Always make sure you are in control, working hard, and pushing forward within your culture of Self Discipline. Be persistent and relentless in your efforts to reach your goals.

12

Mental Toughness

Mental Toughness is the process of maintaining Self Discipline. When the whole world expects you to quit, you don't. When the whole world expects you to drop your standards, you don't. When the world around you burn you still keep on pushing forward. On the surface that is mental toughness.

But mental toughness is a lot deeper than that. It's not just one thing, it's thousands of moments and little choices where you decide to keep going or quit.

Mental Toughness is a term that gets thrown around a lot these days. It's almost a cool thing to talk about. A lot of people make it sound like it's something you can get like a commodity. But the truth is that mental toughness is not just something you acquire once and you're done. It gets developed through backbreaking hard work. It gets forged in the deepest parts of your being. There in the deepest corners of your body, mind, and soul, your mental toughness gets sculpted. You sculpt it like an artist sculpts a statue. It's a process.

How does this process look?

How do you build mental toughness?

(1)You need to Go back and face your past

Now the first reaction from a lot of guys is "wait a minute John, what does my past have to do with my mental toughness and self-discipline?"

My answer? "Everything".

I have mentioned before that everything is connected. When it comes to things like mental toughness and self-discipline your past plays a massive role in your development.

So the next question is why is it important? Well, we all have a past and a story. That story we tell ourselves has played a massive role in our development, mindset, weaknesses, and strengths. It has influenced the way we see ourselves and what we believe is possible.

The truth of those things in our past is that they return to haunt us in the times when we should be at our best. These bad things that happened to us form bad mental habits. For example, maybe you had a big relationship disappointment like a bad breakup. That breakup made you stop believing in yourself and you started to tell yourself you are not good enough. Now a year later in a very challenging time in your business that wound still haunts you. Why? Because you never took time out to face it and deal with it and take responsibility for it.

Most people live life in denial and blame other people for their past. We drag these negative things with us. The results are that we lose our confidence and self-belief.

We need to confront our past so we don't drag it with us. When we are free from those things we get stronger, more confident, and focused on our future.

After we face our past, we cut it loose and let it go. It's done, we learned from it and got stronger. We don't blame anyone for anything. We take full responsibility for our past and future.

(2)Observing The Choices We Make Every day

Life is a very long series of choices, Every choice you make has a domino effect. Every effect has a cause.

-What time do you get up?
   -What do you eat every day?
   -Do you exercise?
   -What do you eat?
   -Did you make the Sales calls?
   -Did you go to Jiu-Jitsu class?
   -Did You Approach that beautiful girl?
   -How many hours a day do you work?
   -How many hours do you sleep?
   -Do you drink when you know you shouldn't?
   -Did you watch TV last night?
   -How many hours were you on social media?
   -How many interruptions did you allow?

Every day these choices and questions come up. We must ask ourselves this question: **How consistently do we make the best choice?**

When you combine good choices with consistency you get a very powerful and effective combination. These small daily actions and evaluations over long periods of time make a large part of what mental toughness is all about. It's not flashy or glamorous but it has immense power.

Let's take exercise for example. An average person goes to the gym 2 or 3 times week. And when I talk about average I'm talking about the small group that actually goes. Within that group, the person will go 3 times then maybe takes some weeks off because there were some parties and work dinners. Then they will go again the next week twice but won't go the third time because their body is hurting from the last session.

Now let's look at the person with a high level of self-discipline combined with a well-developed level of mental toughness. This person will be in the gym 6 days a week every week for months and only take days off with serious injury or illness. They just keep on grinding. Things like hot or cold weather are irrelevant to them. There is only the weather. They adapt, improvise, and keep on grinding. For the casual observer, it's just that one guy who always shows up. Always grinding. He is absolutely relentless in what he does.

Perseverance

I mentioned the world consistency earlier and consistency is very closely linked with perseverance but with a subtle difference. Perseverance can be defined as "steadfastness in doing something despite difficulty or delay in achieving success."This means that when you are absolutely physically exhausted and mentally drained you still push forward. You claw with your fingernails and drag yourself forward to get that next inch.You know that when you count up all those inches that it's going to make the difference in winning or losing. So you fight for every inch like it's the last one on the planet. You always keep moving forward.

Perseverance is the heart of mental toughness because here is the bottom line: You don't have to do this. You can leave right now. You can stop reading this book or listening to the audio-book. You don't need this self-discipline. All the discomfort and pain. You don't need the early mornings and the late nights. You don't need the healthy food and all the missed holidays and parties. You can let it all stop right now. All you have to do is quit. Just tell yourself it's over. Then it's done. However, the mentally tough person will hear all these little voices in his head and he has heard them thousands of times when he is under pressure. But they don't have power over him anymore. He is now in control. He is now the master of his mind. Sure he goes through hard times, but he perseveres, he gets over obstacles because his purpose and vision for his life is so strong he can't be stopped. He has cultivated mental toughness and an extreme level of self-discipline.

Small Wins

When you start thinking big and going after massive goals you will need to fight and overcome many obstacles. You will get tired and things might seem overwhelming at times. In times of battle think about the next small win. So let's say for example you have a goal of making $30000 a month with your online business. This might seem hard to achieve and that is why many people give up. But a good way to mentally overcome this obstacle is by focusing on getting small wins. For example, selling your first product. That is a small win. Selling your first 100 is a small win. Another example in Jiu-Jitsu is getting your first stripe on your belt is a small win. Getting your second stripe another small win. When you start building these small wins you start creating massive wins.

Patience

In a world of instant gratification where people want things right now, many people live in a fantasy world. A lot of people give up because they lack patience. Patience is such a subtle thing that many people miss it. In my line of work with online businesses, it is very common. For example, people see others making money online and they fall for the marketers selling them on the overnight success stories. Don't fall for this myth of overnight success. It does not exist. The truth is that any success takes time. Sure you can get there reasonably fast but don't expect to become a millionaire in a year. Think big but don't think anything of real value gets created overnight. Part of what mental toughness is about is to quietly go about your business while others are complaining on social media pages about "When will I start making money?".Stay away from these types of toxic mentalities and focus on your mission. Just stay relentless and keep on building your small wins until that stack of small wins turn into a mountain and you get your massive win. Stay hungry and stay patient.

The Shiny Object Syndrome

The shiny object syndrome is when people jump from one thing to another without settling on one thing and becoming good at it. The shiny object syndrome breaks many dreams into tiny pieces and many never recover from it. Personally, I wasted a year chasing after something stupid and then came back on my mission.I'm one of the lucky ones that only lost a year. Others lose a lot more than that and never recover.

The shiny object syndrome is very common in business and entrepreneurial circles. People jump around from one thing to another. For example, a person starts an online consulting business but then jumps into crypto-currencies because that is the "Next big thing".And with this specific example of crypto, we now know a lot of people ended up disappointed. In order to avoid this mind virus, you need to be mentally disciplined and start saying no to a lot of things. Don't fall for these shiny objects. Stay focused and say No. Stay on your mission.

Criticism Is Part Of The Game

The more Self Discipline becomes part of your life the more success you will create. With that success will come criticism. This is part of the reality when you put yourself out there and make some moves. People you never heard of will have opinions about you. That is part of the reality when you become successful. Expect it to come and don't let it get you off your mission. Stay focused.

How Do You React To The World?

The world is going to come at you that is inevitable. The only question is how will you react when it does? Let's look at how you can respond when things don't exactly go your way. How can we control our reactions?

(1)Control your environment. If you know you get angry when you stand in a line at the bank then change it by being proactive. Go early when there are no lines. Then you have controlled the situation.

(2)Reframe your reality. If you feel disappointed because for example, you cannot afford a trip to Spain for the summer, then reframe it by telling yourself that you can take a nice trip in your own country. It's not perfect, but you still got your holiday. You can reframe your reality.

(3)Change your focus. If you go for a drive and compare your car with others and feel negative about your life. Start focusing on what you have compared to the people taking the bus.

(4)Change your response in situations. Everything begins with awareness. If you get angry when someone makes a joke about you, then become aware of this. Then next time it happens, take a couple of deep breaths and react differently. For example, smile and just laugh at the person.

(5)The important thing to remember is that we have a choice how we react in any situation. You have a split second before you react. Take a deep breath and choose wisely.

Changing your mind is a process so be patient and keep working on it.

Conclusion

I want to thank you for reading this book! I sincerely hope that you received value from it!

If you received value from this book, I want to ask you for a favour.Would you be kind enough to leave a review for this book ?

Thank You.

For personal coaching contact John Winters at : johnwinters740@gmail.com

Follow me on Twitter: Follow me on Twitter: @Masculineminds

Other Books:

Alpha Mindset - A Guide For Men: How To Build Self-Confidence, Dream Big, Overcome Fear, And Build Better Relationships

Copyright

trademarks and brands within this book are for clarifying purposes only and are the owned by the owners themselves, not affiliated with this document.

Printed in Great Britain
by Amazon

72900652R00087